THURMAN MUNSON

Rookie of the Year and a Most Valuable Player.
A .300 hitter five times with three consecutive years
  of 100 RBIs.
Captain of a three-time pennant winning and two-
  time World Championship club.

Thurman Munson wanted to be remembered as
a player of the 70's. He will be remembered by his
fans for his hustle, his pride, his determination, his
honesty, his confidence, his dignity and his character.

That's how he was both on and off the field.

THURMAN MUNSON

AN AUTOBIOGRAPHY WITH MARTIN APPEL

tempo books

GROSSET & DUNLAP
A Filmways Company
Publishers ● New York

Cover photo by Mickey Palmer

Back cover photo by Louis Requena

Thurman Munson—An Autobiography
Copyright © 1978 by Thurman Lee Munson and Martin Eliot
Appel
Epilogue copyright © 1979 by Martin Eliot Appel
All Rights Reserved
ISBN: 0-448-17191-1
Library of Congress Catalogue Card Number: 78-8924
Published by arrangement with Coward, McCann &
Geoghegan, Inc.
First paperback edition: May 1980
Tempo Books is registered in the U.S. Patent Office
Published simultaneously in Canada
Printed in the United States of America

To Diane, Tracy, Kelly, and Mike
—T.M.

To Pat
—M.A.

CONTENTS

THURMAN MUNSON

A MIKE GARCIA
AUTOGRAPH

I was glancing through some mail in my locker in Fort Lauderdale Stadium, talking to Graig Nettles about an upcoming fishing contest, when Pete Sheehy slowly approached.

Pete's been the chief of the Yankee clubhouse, both in New York and in Florida, for more than fifty years, and slow is his normal speed. Sometimes, the players refer to him as the grim reaper, for when roster cuts are made, he's usually the man who comes up and says, "They'd like to see you in the office."

Fortunately, I never experienced that feeling, because I was never cut in spring training. The only time I was ever "sent down" was when I was a nonroster player, just invited for a look, with the full understanding that I'd be going to the minor league camp by the end of training camp. So Pete was not the bearer of bad news for me on this March afternoon in 1976, merely the carrier of a message that Billy Martin wanted to see me before I left.

The manager's office is just before the exit, and after I'd dressed, I poked my head in. "You wanted to see me, Billy?"

"Oh, yeh, Thurman, come in," Billy Martin said. "Listen,

George thinks it would be a good idea if we had a captain on the club—you know, sort of an official team leader. And we're agreed that you're the best choice for the job, so I'm appointing you captain. We'll make an official announcement to the press in a few days, but I wanted to let you know myself now."

I looked at him silently for a moment, then sort of shrugged my shoulders and said, "Okay with me. Thanks!" And off I went.

I didn't give it a great deal of thought, and the significance was rather lost on me. I should have realized at the time what must have been going through Billy's mind. He had played with Mickey Mantle, Joe DiMaggio, Yogi Berra, Whitey Ford, Phil Rizzuto—the greatest stars—and none had ever been a captain. In fact, Billy himself might have been the best choice of them all, because as a player, he was considered the on-field leader of the team.

As I later learned, none of those men had been named captains because the position had been "retired." When captain Lou Gehrig had died in 1941, Joe McCarthy, his manager, had declared that out of respect for Lou no one would ever hold the office again.

Now George Steinbrenner, who loves the Yankee tradition and history, decided the time had come to break that tradition and name a captain. George's first sports experiences were in football, and I'm sure that helped influence his feelings. Furthermore, having a captain rather enhanced the total prestige of the organization. So at the time, I felt the move was at least somewhat for the benefit of the owner. Don't get me wrong—I was honored. But the history of the assignment was lost on me, and I didn't appreciate it as I might have.

I remember that a few days later Yogi came up to me and said, "Thurman, you've become the best hitter in the league with men on base." Now, *that's* an honor, having a guy as great as Yogi pay me a compliment like that. There's nothing like respect from your peers, and I guess I didn't feel that way about being named captain.

But in all honesty, even Lou Gehrig didn't mean that much to me. Oh, I knew him from the *Pride of the Yankees* movie, and I was able to associate him with Babe Ruth, but I could never tell you if he was ever MVP, if he ever led the league in home runs, or what number he wore. I was just never that much of a fan, where things like that registered. In fact, if I wasn't a Yankee, I'd still be in the dark about the game's past. On the Yankees, one can't help but get an education, because the team is so rich in history.

As the season went on and everyone began making a big deal about my being captain, it began to have more meaning for me. And eventually, the pride which should have been there at the start grew. I now know who Lou Gehrig is, and while I don't think being captain made me a better player, or even a better leader, I'm touched by the honor of being associated with him.

I was the youngest of four children in my family. First came two sisters, Darla and Janice, then a brother, Duane, and on June 7, 1947, there was me. I once asked my dad why he named me Thurman Lee Munson, and he told me I was named after some athlete named Thurman Lee, but I never have found out who this Thurman Lee fellow was. And even though my name doesn't exactly roll off the tongue, it's hard to forget once you've heard it, and no one has ever come up with a nickname which stuck.

When I was four, we moved from my birthplace in Akron, Ohio, to a farm in a town called Randolph, out in the country. There was a lot of room to play ball there, and I began to learn baseball from Duane and my dad, Darrell. Duane was a good athlete, but never took it very seriously, and certainly never thought of it in terms of being a professional.

My dad, though, probably would have had the drive to be

a pro if he had had the inclination. I mean, he was the world's original hard-nosed competitor. I'm sure that's where I inherited my desire from. Dad would think nothing of hitting us ground balls for hours, and if one took a bad hop and bloodied a nose, he'd just go right on hitting without stopping.

When I started to play in organized games, I could go four for four, and he'd get all over me afterward for some fielding lapse. To friends and neighbors, he'd always be building me up, but it was sure tough to drag a compliment out of him directly. He even had a similar relationship with my mom, Ruth. When Dad was around, everyone in the house, including Mom, was intimidated. It seemed as though her chief responsibility was to keep us out of trouble so that Dad wouldn't get mad at us.

Mom was also a great cook, which was no small necessity in the Munson home. We all had good appetites, and fortunately for me, I never had a real weight problem. In fact, right into my sophomore year of high school, I weighed only 125 pounds.

The farm was fun, but a few years later we moved to Canton, Ohio, where we rented a small house. I shared a bed with Duane. I remember thinking we were on the border of the "rich section" of town, where homes could go for $30,000. I loved Canton, because there were always so many guys to play ball with. On the farm, it was Dad, Duane, and I, and if one of us was missing, you couldn't have much of a workout. But in Canton, there was always the opportunity to get a quick pickup game going in the streets. We'd play Wiffle ball, sockball, softball—you name it.

Canton was the town in which Cy Young began his professional career back in 1890. His name was Denton Young, but when he came to Canton for a tryout, they had him pitch against a wooden fence. He chipped away at that wood with his fastball, so they say, and someone remarked that "it looks like a cyclone hit that fence." So he became "Cy" Young in Canton.

But Canton, and for that matter most of Ohio, really grew into a hotbed of football country. When it came to talking about sports, it was football, football, football. I can't even remember the Indians winning the American League pennant in 1954, even though I was old enough to have noticed. I was a big Cleveland Browns fan, though, and remember them winning year after year in the old American Conference. And today, of course, Canton is the home of the Professional Football Hall of Fame. But, sorry to say, I've never even been there. I was really a poor excuse for a fan, I suppose.

Take autographs, for example. There was something that I could never understand. Even today, I can't see why somebody couldn't just shake your hand and say hello. The autograph, I know, serves as proof that you really met so-and-so, and in New York, the kids probably do a big business selling them, but to me, they just don't have much meaning.

Well, wait a minute, now. I guess I'm not being entirely honest there. I remember the first autograph I ever got. It was on a rare trip to Municipal Stadium in Cleveland, when Dad was available to take us there. Dad was a long-distance trucker, and he really didn't have a lot of time to cart us off to Cleveland. But on this one particular day, we were sitting down the left field line when Mike Garcia, the big Cleveland pitcher, came walking by.

I called down to Mike and asked for a baseball. He surprised me by getting one, and before he tossed it up, I asked him to sign it. I still have that ball.

And I've got a catcher's mitt signed in white by a lot of the Yankee old-timers, which I've put in a display case at home. And I've got a Mickey Mantle autograph. So perhaps I'm being a little harsh on other autograph seekers, after all.

My family didn't have a lot of money, although we never thought of ourselves as poor. When I was old enough, I got my first glove, a Hutch model, which gave me a lot of good use as I entered grade school at the Worley School.

The Canton school system had a good sports program, and both Duane and I started to earn certificates of recognition at young ages. Baseball was not the biggest sport in the community, but it was the one I enjoyed the most. Football and basketball games, at the high school level, were played on weekends or evenings, and drew big crowds. Baseball games were after-school affairs, and never drew more than a few hundred spectators. But I really loved to play that game.

By the time I got to Lehman High School, I was participating in all three major sports. The Lehman Polar Bears were able to field good teams in most sports, and by the time I was a senior, I was the captain of all three. I was a halfback and a linebacker in football, and a guard in basketball. I had some all-city and all-state honors in those sports, and earned three letters in each.

In baseball, I was a four-letter man. Our coach was Don Eddins, a real driver and a hustler. He taught me a lot about the game, and I enjoyed playing for him. I pitched a few games for Lehman, and caught a couple, but shortstop was my primary position, and it was as a shortstop that I was named All-Ohio in 1965, following a .581 season at the plate. It was certainly during those years that I made up my mind that I was going to be a professional baseball player, and I never lacked the confidence from then on. That confidence, which some people think is cockiness, has never been far from me, and I know it's made me a better player.

Baseball occupied my summers once I reached high school age, for I joined the Canton City Baseball League, a well-organized amateur circuit with schedules of forty or more games a year. To many, it was a good extension of the fine Little League and Pony League programs Canton

offered. To me, it was a chance to keep playing even after
school ended each June.

I played for the Seran Agency in the Canton City Baseball League, and in three summers had batting averages of
.372, .381, and .441. Shortstop was still my main position,
but again I'd catch a little, and pitch on occasion, and usually batted third in the lineup.

Several times, our team went to the American Amateur
Baseball Congress national tournament in Battle Creek,
Michigan. I did well in those series, and the games gave me
the opportunity to size up the competition from outside the
Canton area. Since I was able to hold my own against ev-
eryone, my confidence was further reinforced.

School was fun for me. I was a little mischievous, perhaps, but I wasn't too bad a student. I liked English and history, and didn't care much for the maths or sciences. That
seems odd to me today, because now I really enjoy math. I
handle most of my own business affairs, and am quite adept
at figures. But it wasn't until college that my aptitude
moved in that direction.

Would you believe that Thurman Munson wrote poetry
in high school? It's true, and I don't mean *Casey at the Bat,*
either. I'd write about children, or God, or things that required some sensitivity. I was rather proud of my efforts.

School was also important to me for another reason.
That's where Diana Dominick was.

I was only twelve when I met Diana. We were both on Ju-
nior Patrol in grade school, helping to get the younger children across the streets. I'm sure she considered me cocky
even at that age, but I could tell she liked me, and for all in-
tents and purposes, we were the only boyfriend/girlfriend
each other ever had, which is pretty unusual these days.

At first, I was a challenge to Diana, because I was a better athlete than she was. And she was pretty good, too. I remember her tagging along on my paper route after school
when I'd deliver the Canton *Repository,* and how she'd al-

ways keep up with me on her bike. She was a "rich kid" to me, because her parents would give her thirty cents a day for spending money, and I didn't get any. She'd spend the money buying me potato chips and Coke and things, which, if you look at it now, was not a bad investment.

I can remember running a mile to Diana's house during baseball training, giving her a kiss, and running back to mine. Not a bad way to get my running in.

Diana's parents always liked me, although my parents, being of German stock, were far more reserved in their approach to Diana, and seemed far more concerned with whether she was occupying too much of my time. But they weren't at all hostile to her, just a bit unresponsive.

Diana, her parents, my parents, my baseball coach, and I all agreed that college was the right move for me. But I knew I could go only if I could get a scholarship, because there was no way my parents could afford it.

I got about eighty letters from colleges expressing an interest in me for their football programs, including Kansas, Ohio State, Syracuse, and Michigan. But it was baseball that I wanted, and schools just aren't that interested in awarding baseball scholarships. I wound up with exactly three offers.

Arizona State, the nation's top baseball college, offered me a scholarship based on making the team. Ohio University offered me a half-scholarship, contingent on making the starting team. I had no doubts that I could accomplish that, but it was Kent State, in Kent, Ohio, that offered me a full scholarship, no strings attached, and that was where I decided to go.

KENT STATE

My college years were four of the most worthwhile years of my life. In all ways—socially, academically, and athletically—they were years of rapid maturity, and I look back on them today as one great experience.

Naturally, I had some mixed emotions about leaving Diana back in Canton, but Kent wasn't very far away, and I'd be able to see her often.

This was the first time I'd ever be away from home for anything longer than a baseball road trip, and I really looked forward to that. When you get out of high school, you never seem to think about all of the basic, adult things you've yet to try—like getting a place to live, handling finances, arranging travel, adjusting to roommates, etc. They're not very serious problems, but college is the first opportunity for most people to work them out, and the growth experience was very rewarding for me.

I lived in a dormitory for all four years at Kent, and always had the same roommate. I couldn't afford an apartment, and I was perfectly content to live in the dorm. I joined Delta Upsilon fraternity, enrolled as a business ma-

17

jor, and signed up to play freshman basketball and baseball.

Kent State is a large college, made up primarily of Ohio
students. Despite a student enrollment of over 10,000, it
was never a major athletic power, and did not become a na-
tionally known institution until the tragic events of 1970,
when four students were shot and killed by Ohio National
Guardsmen during a student demonstration.

The campus was a quiet one when I was there, and even
if it had been active, I doubt if I would have gotten involved. I'm not a very politically minded person, and particularly in those days, my mind was really all on sports.

Now, I really feel bad about the events which occurred
there after I had departed. The killings, aside from the awful cost of four lives, brought a lot of shame to the school
and tainted an otherwise fine reputation. In 1977, trouble
erupted again when the university decided to build a gym
near the site of the killings. I tended to side with the students here. I mean, we used to play football in the parking
lot right next to the site, and when I think about what happened, I get a chill. I think a fitting memorial to the slain
students would be entirely appropriate, and I'm sorry to see
the zeal with which the college officials pursue the gym-
nasium. Joan Baez, the folksinger, called me not long ago
seeking my support on the matter.

Anyway, all of that happened two years after I'd left
Kent, so I wasn't really close enough to the situation to get
more deeply involved.

What I really cared about was baseball. I started college
still considered a shortstop, but by now my weight was a
solid 195, and I'd been getting more and more experience
behind the plate.

Back in high school, there was a pitcher who threw so
hard no one could catch him except me. That's where my
first experience developed. No one ever really taught me
how to catch, and I just let the development come naturally.

Besides, defense wasn't that important to me then. I just loved to hit, and it didn't matter to me where I played in the field.

Our freshman baseball schedule called for eleven games, but we had just awful weather in the spring of 1965, and wound up playing only three. I caught them all and batted .416, but as far as I was concerned, it was a wasted year. It's not hard to understand why so many of today's draft picks come from the California-Arizona area. People can play ball year round there. In the Northeast, we're limited to whatever breaks the weather gives us.

I spent the summer after my freshman year back in the Canton City Baseball League, and returned for my sophomore year prepared for varsity baseball. These days, you can play varsity for four years, but back then, you had to devote your freshman season to the freshman team.

Dick "Moose" Paskert was the baseball coach at Kent, and a real veteran he was. He had already coached for nineteen years when I got there, and his reputation was strong in the Mid-Atlantic Conference. I liked Moose a great deal. He was not only a fine coach, but he was always coming up with gimmicks for our club, like selling key chains or things to get money for our northern trip. A real promoter, and just a helluva guy.

He had coached two previous players who went on to the big leagues—Rich Rollins, the fine third baseman whose best years were with Minnesota, and Gene Michael, who later became my roommate on the Yankees. Leave it to Moose, all of our bats were either Michael or Rollins models, too.

Michael would work out at Kent sometimes during his off-seasons, and I got to know him a bit then. I never imagined myself as a future teammate, though.

I made some changes in my sophomore year. First, I abandoned basketball, deciding to devote all of my energies to baseball. And then I switched my major from business to health education, with an eye toward a teaching degree in case I needed something to fall back on some day. Michael had earned a teaching degree when he was a Kent student, and had even gone on to do substitute teaching when his baseball schedule allowed.

Unfortunately, switching my major slowed my progress toward a degree, and I lost a number of credits. It made it impossible for me to graduate in four years, and I wound up some thirty credits short. I went back for more classes after my first year of pro ball, but then it just became impossible, with spring training starting in February for batterymen, and I never managed to finish.

Under Paskert in my sophomore year, I became an everyday catcher. The best pitcher on the team was Steve Stone, who later signed with the Giants, and had some good seasons for the White Sox and the Cubs. Steve and I became good friends, and remain so even now as we oppose each other from time to time.

The Kent State Flashes never won the conference title while I was there, but we had some good seasons, and scouts began watching us. I never doubted I was going to play in the majors one day soon.

I went home to the Canton League for the summer of 1967 and got a job as a house painter to earn some money. Not long into June, I was asked if I'd be interested in playing in the Cape Cod League. It seemed the Chatham team's catcher had been injured, and my name had been mentioned as a good replacement.

The Cape Cod League was one of six summer leagues in the United States financially aided by the major leagues, providing summer baseball programs for college players. Besides Chatham, the Cape Cod League was made up of Falmouth, Cotuit, Bourne, Wareham, Orleans, Yarmouth, and Harwich. Joe Lewis was manager at Chatham, and I earned $75 a week working for the Chatham parks department. It was the best money I'd ever earned, and the league

was a good one. I wound up winning the Most Valuable
Player award, too, hitting .420, which was 65 points higher
than the runner-up, Glenn Adams, who later played for the
Twins. And Chatham won the championship with a 30-9
record.

Back for my senior year at Kent, I really couldn't wait for
baseball season. I did my work and got decent grades, but
my mind was on the game, and many was the day I wished
we *were* in Southern California, playing ball all year.

Not surprising to me, the scouts began to show up with
regularity at our games. I never knew them by name, or
even by team, for that matter, unless someone pointed
them out, but you couldn't miss them as a group—all sitting together, holding little notepads, and writing down ob-
servations.

We were well scouted on Cape Cod, where Yankee scout
Harry Hesse first saw me play. Harry was an old-timer who
really *looked* like a baseball scout. He was based in New
York, but the Yankees assigned him to our league that
summer, and with all the potentially good prospects there,
it was obvious they thought a good deal of his abilities.

Through the Yankee office, Hesse passed on word about
me, and during my senior year at Kent, Gene Woodling began to watch me regularly.

Gene was more obvious than other scouts, because he was
a former big league star. Moose would point him out to me
when he'd show up. Now, I know that scouts are only supposed to have the minimal contact with you, but Woodling
really used to frustrate me. He'd never say a word to me.
Just show up, take his seat, and take his notes. Never a hello or anything. I'm a talkative guy, and would have enjoyed
having a conversation with him, but I never could get one
going. When the day finally came where he introduced himself, I acted as if I hadn't been aware of his presence all
along.

Of course, there were other scouts, too. I know the Indians' scout wrote me off because he said I couldn't run. But I knew I was making an impression, and if they didn't notice it right away on the playing field, they couldn't help but notice it on the statistics sheet.

In my senior year at Kent, I played in twenty-five league games, scored twenty-four runs, and drove in thirty. I had nineteen extra-base hits, stole nine bases, and batted .413. I walked twenty-four times and struck out only three times. I was, as they say, really making contact.

At the end of the season, I was named All-American as catcher. To this day, that remains one of the greatest moments in my life. When you think of the fact that there are some 5,000 major colleges in the United States, and I was the one man named as catcher, it's really some honor. I mean, as great as winning the MVP Award was with the Yankees eight years later, the competition was against only 300 other American Leaguers. And as far as winning Rookie of the Year in 1970, how many rookies were there? But All-American was really something!

It was a decent All-American team that came out of colleges that year. Steve Garvey of Michigan State was the third baseman, and Elliott Maddox of Michigan was in the outfield. Dave Lemonds, Rich McKinney, Tom Paciorek, Sandy Vance, and Tom Bradley were also All-American.

As I said, my plans were to continue on with college, although, of course, my four years of eligibility were up. I figured I'd be drafted, but had no idea of where or by whom. The free agent draft system was only four years old at that point, and hadn't been around long enough to become predictable.

So I went home to Canton, spent time with Diana, and prepared to return to Cape Cod for another summer league. I left on June 6, which was the day of the draft, and the day before my twenty-first birthday. There was no reason not to go, because even if I was drafted, I could still play there all summer and sign at a later date. I had no preconceived notions, and just waited to see what happened.

I went to Cape Cod with John Curtis, the pitcher who also reached the majors, and who at the time was also playing in that league. I'd only been up there a few hours when my sister called, telling me that I'd been selected fourth in the nation, and picked by the New York Yankees.

The first pick in the country was made by the New York Mets, and they took infielder Tim Foli. Oakland drafted second and went for Dartmouth's Pete Broberg. But Broberg didn't sign with them, and waited until 1971 before signing with Washington.

Houston had the third pick, and took a catcher named Martin Cott, who never reached the majors. In fact, I think his last effort was in the Yankee farm system before he hung 'em up.

Then the Yankees picked me, and I understand that Gene Woodling's scouting report was all crossed off and replaced by two words—"GET HIM."

Well, not long after my sister called, I got a call from Lee MacPhail, the Yankees' general manager. And after speaking for just a few minutes, we knew we were going to do some business very soon.

So without even having unpacked, I flew right home to Canton. There were happy faces waiting for me at home— my whole family, Diana and her whole family. We all had a sense that I was about to embark on an exciting new life.

Lee MacPhail arrived the next day, and we all met at my parents' home. Gene Woodling was there, too. I liked Lee the first time I met him, and my respect for him never wavered. He was, of course, an employee of the ball club, and his job was to make the best deal he could on behalf of that club. But he had an honesty and an integrity about him, and I felt that there would never be a question of trust here. I knew that it wouldn't be necessary to put it all in writing, look for loopholes, etc. He was, and is, a decent man.

My parents sensed it, too, and we didn't have a great deal of trouble coming to terms. Although estimates of my bonus ranged well over six figures, it was actually closer to

$75,000, and included payment for the remainder of my education. Sure, you look back and always think you could have made a better deal, but I was pleased then, and I'm still pleased with the way I handled myself in my first experience.

MacPhail's father, now in the Hall of Fame, was a flamboyant showman, and, of course, a good businessman, too, who held charge over the Reds, the Dodgers, and the Yankees during his career. I never met him, but I'm told he would think nothing of getting into a fistfight to prove a point. He was loud, obvious, and exciting. Lee was anything but. It was hard to believe they were related, let alone in the same profession. I'm sure Lee heard that a thousand times from people who knew his father.

MacPhail used to kid that Gene Michael was a great negotiator, and if he ever needed his own contract negotiated, he'd hire Gene. All I can say is that Lee never had a chance to deal with me when I reached my prime in negotiating. We would have had some terrific sessions, I can assure you. Perhaps it's for the best that he moved on before those days arrived, and that we both remain genuinely fond of each other.

Interestingly, the only man who ever got a six-figure signing bonus from the Yankees was Jake Gibbs, whom I succeeded as the team's regular catcher.

I know a lot of kids will get that big bonus and run out and buy cars and clothes and everything they always had to shop carefully for. But that wasn't my ambition.

My bonus was paid in two equal installments, and after taxes were deducted from the first half, I couldn't believe how little was left. Still, I had my heart set on an acre and a quarter of commercially zoned land in Canton, and borrowed against the rest of my bonus to purchase it. People said I paid more than it was worth, and maybe I did, being inexperienced, but eleven months later, I sold it for a profit of $12,000!

So I was a landowner and a baseball player. My signing with the Yankees called for $500 a month to play for Binghamton, New York, in the Eastern League. It was a Double-A classification, one of the things I specified to Lee. I didn't want to start lower than Double-A, and Gene Woodling backed up my confidence, telling Lee that I could play in the big leagues in two years.

I packed my clothes (I was as bad a dresser then as I am now), packed my baseball gear, checked on my real estate, said good-bye to everyone, and headed for Binghamton. I was about to become a professional baseball player.

"MICKEY, I'M THURMAN MUNSON"

Without a doubt, the Binghamton Triplets had the worst clubhouse I'd ever seen, and I wouldn't be surprised if it was the worst one in all of professional baseball. I mean, there were holes in the floor! We couldn't wait to get onto the field. Maybe that was the idea.

It was not much of a first impression as I arrived in the small city, about thirty miles north of the Pennsylvania border. But I was still excited about embarking on this new phase of my life, and since everyone on the club made light of the conditions and tended to joke about them, I felt at ease and joined in.

Our trainer that year was Gene Monahan, who later moved up and became the trainer on the Yankees. We were the last survivors of the 1968 Binghamton Triplets, for by 1977, everyone else on the roster had been released or had quit. Steve Kline was the last to go, a sore arm finally bringing his career to a close in '77. Other players who had at least a cup of coffee in the biggies from that team included Frank Tepedino, a Brooklyn-born first baseman who

26

could really hit, and Gary Jones, a pitcher who came up to the Yankees late one season and got into a couple of games.

My best friend on the team was another first baseman, Tim O' Connell, who later was an usher at my wedding. Otherwise, it's almost hard to remember the names of the other players. Our manager was Cloyd Boyer, a fine gentleman, and the older brother of Ken and Clete. "C.B.," as he was known long before anyone used the term for radios, was really the Yankees' minor league pitching coach, but was serving a managerial stint that year at Binghamton.

I liked Boyer, and was happy for him nine years later when he finally got a chance to return to the major leagues as the Yankees' pitching coach. There are a lot of guys in baseball like Boyer, who spend two or three decades of their lives serving an organization in the minor leagues without ever getting any pension benefits. Some, like Earl Weaver, Tom Lasorda, and Frank Lucchesi, eventually get a big league managing job. And on occasion, as was the case with Boyer, the organization rewards him by letting him get some pension time in. (A man needs four years in the majors to qualify for a pension.)

Boyer, having been a pitcher, was naturally great for a pitching staff, but he was a help to me as well, and he bolstered my confidence by telling me that I could probably play in the big leagues within a year.

I had really set no timetable for myself in that regard, but, obviously, I was eager to make the trip up as quickly as possible. That remains a big difference today between the baseball and football structures, and explains partially why at times baseball will lose a great prospect to pro football. No matter how big a star you might have been in college, no matter how big a bonus you might have received, in baseball you start out at places like Binghamton, and in football you generally start out right at the top. The thought of three or four years of long bus rides, low meal money, bad clubhouses, and low salary, has definitely influenced some players to play football, where they can at least find out right away whether they're going to make it in the pros or not.

But I don't want to put minor league ball down. After all, baseball is baseball, and if you love to play the game, then once that first pitch is thrown, it doesn't matter much where you're playing. It's a super game to play, and a great way to make a living. Maybe you can get a little spoiled after a few years in the majors, but, basically, give me a uniform, hand me a bat, and I'm one happy guy.

If I had any doubts about being able to hold my own in pro baseball, they didn't have time to get me down, because I started hitting right away and never faltered. The quality of the pitching didn't bother me, for it wasn't that much superior to what I'd seen in Cape Cod or even at Kent. More pitchers could throw well, but few were better than the best I'd seen previously, so there was no major adjustment necessary for me. And while I was certainly taking my catching responsibilities more seriously and working on throwing more, I was still a hitter at heart, and loved taking my turn at bat.

Even then, it was my throwing arm that people mostly spoke of when they talked about my catching. I always had a strong arm, going back to my days as a shortstop, but a strong arm doesn't mean anything if you don't have accuracy. That was what I worked on, and that's what fell into place for me. I still had good reflexes and good speed, and really enjoyed the challenge of throwing out runners. In fact, if there was a short passed ball or a wild pitch, I'd enjoy the added challenge of recovering the ball and still getting my man.

The year 1968 was a year of great political turmoil in the country, and the war in Vietnam was raging at full strength. The army and the draft were very much on the minds of guys my age. In the middle of the 1968 season, the

Yankees sought to get me enrolled in a reserve unit in Fort Lauderdale, where the major league club trained. I flew down there and was met at the airport by Ed Bastian, the general manager of the Yankees' entry in the Florida State League.

The army post was directly next to Fort Lauderdale Stadium, so my first look at the beautiful facility came many months before my first spring training. But it was worth only a glance to me, for my mind was much on the physical and what it might mean to my baseball career.

I didn't pass. An extra bone spur in my right ankle was enough to flunk me, and, much relieved, I went back to Binghamton and rejoined the Triplets.

The absence cost me a few games, and probably the Eastern League batting title. I wound up my rookie year with a .301 average, making me the only .300 in the league. Unfortunately, I missed qualifying by about ten trips to the plate.

I got into seventy-one games and had 226 at bats, hitting six homers and driving in thirty-seven runs. They were good statistics for a rookie, particularly a number one draft choice whom everyone would be watching.

The highlight of the season for me was an exhibition game we played at Yankee Stadium in August. It was the only time in my memory that the Yankees invited a minor league affiliate to play in the big ball park. We were having a series with Waterbury, a Cleveland farm club based in Connecticut. We bused it into the Bronx, and it was my first visit ever to both New York City and to Yankee Stadium.

Of course, we didn't see any of New York City, for the stadium is north of Manhattan and across a river. And we bused it right out after the game.

But Yankee Stadium was magnificent. Three decks, all painted in dark blue, contrasted with a bright white exterior. The place had been completely repainted the year before, and, as historic as it was, it had a fresh glisten to it.

Some of the Triplets made their way out to the monuments in center field, others just sat in the dugout and stared up at the high stands. Me, I went over to say hello to Mickey Mantle.

Now, I said that I was never a hero-worshiper, but Mickey was an exception. If you grew up in the fifties and sixties, there was no escaping him. There were Mickey Mantle T-shirts, and Mickey Mantle bats, and Mickey Mantle gloves. And there was Mickey every October hitting World Series home runs. I always thought that if you went to a foreign country and someone asked you who the greatest sports hero in America was, Mickey would sound like a Hollywood creation, with those looks, that name, and that talent. I don't think anyone in baseball ever had his combination of power and speed, and he was a switch-hitter to boot.

So even if I wasn't a big fan, I had to love Mickey Mantle. And here was my first chance to see him in person. We were teammates, sort of. Well, at least my bonus check and his weekly check both said "New York Yankees."

At the time, no one knew that 1968 would be Mickey's last season as a player, probably not even Mickey. And although he was only a shade of his former self at bat in terms of average, he still led the club in home runs and in game-winning hits that season, a real tribute to his ability.

I was pretty nervous—even shaking—as I walked over to him, but I tried to act casual and polite, and I simply extended my hand and said, "Mickey, I'm Thurman Munson." Since I was in my Binghamton uniform, I didn't think it was necessary to say what I was doing there, and I didn't think it was necessary to say I was the team's number one draft choice last month or anything like that. Mickey gave me a firm hand shake, a friendly smile, and a "how ya doin'," which was enough to satisfy me. It was a terrific thrill, and, looking back now, I really regret that I missed by just one year having him as a teammate. Everyone who ever played with Mickey always spoke so well of him.

I went onto the field, and there were a few spectators around—probably more than we usually drew in the Eastern League, but a small-looking crowd inside the 65,000 capacity Yankee Stadium.

I took a few swings, and then a photographer took my picture. I think he was the Yankees' photographer, and, since he took only myself and Steve Kline, I felt pretty important, as though he was shooting on orders from top. Of course, that was probably my imagination.

Gene Michael was with the Yankees then, and I of course knew him from when he'd work out at Kent State. We exchanged some pleasantries, and he sat in the Yankee dugout during our game. Other Yankees were watching, too—Mel Stottlemyre, Fritz Peterson, Rocky Colavito, Bobby Cox, Jake Gibbs, Lindy McDaniel, and some I didn't recognize. Once the game started, though, I was just doing what came naturally, and I remember with satisfaction getting a double. I figured somewhere upstairs Lee MacPhail and Ralph Houk were probably watching.

In August, Diana came up to Binghamton with her mother for a weekend visit. It was there and then that we got engaged. I suppose we always knew we would—we'd been talking about getting married since we were about thirteen. We set the wedding date for September 21, shortly after the season would end. The reason for that was that this time I really felt I'd be headed for the army. Flunked physical or not, my draft number had come up, and the extra spur might not keep me out a second time. So, feeling certain that I'd be off to the army quickly, we decided to get married before rather than after.

We had a nice wedding, with Diana's big family and my small family, some of my buddies, and good food. The newspaper said quite formally, "Mr. Munson is a professional baseball player in the New York Yankees' organization," the way those wedding notices are always prepared. We took off for a terrific honeymoon in Hawaii, and I still expected to be called into duty any day. I had passed the second physical, this one in Cleveland.

We got back from Hawaii and moved in with Diana's parents, not sure what we were awaiting. With no army call coming, I registered for some additional credits at Kent State, but they were the last ones I was to get. With spring training coming in mid-February for pitchers and catchers, it was almost impossible to work out a normal class schedule, and I abandoned the idea after that one winter. That's one reason I really respect the effort that George Medich had to put in toward earning his medical degree while pursuing his baseball career.

The winter came and went, the army didn't call, and it was time for another season. For 1969, I was promoted to the Syracuse Chiefs, the top Yankee farm club, members of the International League. And my letter for spring training told me that I was to report to the major league camp in Fort Lauderdale as a non-roster catcher.

RESERVE DUTY

I couldn't wait to get going in 1969, and was glad when February finally arrived. Pitchers and catchers always report four or five days before the rest of the squad for spring training, because the pitchers need the extra days to work their arms into condition, and, as Casey Stengel once said, "Without the catchers, you'd have all passed balls."

The team normally invites two or three non-roster catchers to camp, primarily to assist with the warmup responsibilities of the twenty or so pitchers. It is always made perfectly clear that there will be no chance to make the team, thereby avoiding a letdown when you report to the minor league camp. From time to time, a non-roster pitcher might make the club, as Fred Beene did with us one season, but it's really quite unusual, particularly among catchers. So I made up my mind that I was here to handle the pitchers, nothing else, but that I'd make the most of my chances in the batting cage. And obviously, as the team's top draft choice the year before, there would certainly be an interest in observing me.

The coaching staff was newsworthy in 1969. Dick Howser

had become the team's third base coach, moving up from the ranks of the players and replacing Frank Crosetti, a fixture with the Yankees for decades. And Elston Howard was back, named by the Yankees as the first black coach in the American League. Ellie had played for the Yankees from 1955-1967, when he was traded to Boston and helped them win a pennant. He was promised that there would always be a place for him in the Yankee organization when he retired, and the Yankees were true to their word. As a former catcher, Ellie would be of help to me, as would Jim Hegan, the bullpen coach and another catching veteran of the American League. Hegan had been a Yankee coach since 1960.

The pitching coach was Jim Turner, "the colonel," as everyone called him. He was a real student of the game, and probably Ralph Houk's most trusted lieutenant. Whitey Ford was in spring training as a special instructor, so it was certainly a star-studded faculty.

Whitey was the most natural guy you could ever meet. Some people who attain the heights of greatness in their fields can develop an aloof quality, and even while outwardly seeking friendliness, display the air of being somewhat above you. Ford never demonstrated that weakness. Any laughs were always on himself, and while he certainly had an awareness of his place in the sport, he had the style of humility that put everyone at ease. He was a very easy guy to like.

The natural charm gave him a gift for talking to athletes that very few people have. In short, Whitey could tell a player he was lousy without hurting his feelings. I don't mean as blatantly as that—Whitey was so smooth he'd tell it to the player and the guy would never know what he was really hearing. But later on, the message would sink in with no bad feelings at all. Whitey was giving a rookie a message either that baseball would never be a way to a living for him or that he had better shape up and work on that one big flaw, or he'd never reach the majors. Not many people can deal with these career-making situations with Whitey's poise.

I had met Ralph Houk very briefly during the Binghamton exhibition the summer before, but I looked forward to getting to know him better now that I was in training camp. He had a tremendous reputation among the players, and turned out to be one of the finest men I've ever known in my life.

Among the fans, he had a really tough image, nurtured by his World War II heroics and his gruff appearance, particularly when he'd take on an umpire and dropkick his cap in anger. But he was in fact one of the most sensitive and understanding people I've ever known. He was a man who could earn equally high respect from religious people like Bobby Richardson or Lindy McDaniel, to the more carefree and reckless sorts like Joe Pepitone.

He was a lenient man, but made his rules stick by earning that respect. If the rule was to wear a tie on the road, and a player didn't, Ralph would make some small remark, with a smile, like "Nice tie today," or something equally trite, which would at once show the player that the rule was to be enforced while maintaining a shared understanding that this wasn't the world's greatest tragedy, but let's go along with it.

If a player made a mistake on the field, Ralph would always wait a day and then talk to the player privately in his office. There were never any public fines or public criticisms. The writers used to get on Ralph for being overoptimistic or for standing up for even the worst players, but he was loyal to the team and to the organization, and, after all, that was where his loyalties belonged.

He had an excellent working relationship with Lee Mac-Phail, and the two never got in each other's way. They were frequent dinner companions, and I'm sure would hack up the team pretty good over a meal. But never was a criticism carried beyond their private conversations.

The third member of the Yankee leadership at the time was the team's president, Mike Burke. I never really knew Mike at all, other than to exchange hellos when he'd come around. One time, I asked him to see if he might be able to get someone to mount an award for me. I think that was the only conversation of substance we ever had.

I remember that Mike would sometimes take infield practice in spring training, wearing his street clothes. It was kind of funny, but he wouldn't make a big deal of it—just enough to make sure the newsmen got the story.

Mike was a CBS vice-president, and in those years when I first signed, the club was owned by the television network. It was the only corporate-owned team in baseball, but, as players, we didn't feel any difference. It was as though Mike himself owned the team as far as we were concerned, and the CBS influence was hardly felt at all.

I'm sure the presence was felt in the office. CBS had purchased the prestigious Yankees in 1964, when the club was winning its fifth straight pennant. Then the bottom fell out, and for years the corporation was stuck with mediocre teams—hardly the prestige they were looking for.

Burke, though, made a sizable contribution. The Yankees, during their winning days, had a terrible image among the fans. As many would show up to root against them as root for them. Everyone likes an underdog, and in the case of playing the Yankees, everyone else was an underdog.

Then the Yankees developed a manner about them which was considered stuffy and aloof. They were not the "team of the people," as the old Brooklyn Dodgers had been. They were more the team for the wealthy season box holders.

Burke, assisted somewhat by infrequent winning, turned that around. It was hard to find the proverbial Yankee-haters any more. Maybe the Mets owned the town, and maybe the fans weren't pouring out to see the Yankees play, but that cold corporate image was fading, and Burke, a smart public relations man, was largely responsible. So he did his part, as MacPhail did his, as Houk did his. It was a well-run organization.

Houk ran a good spring training camp, and, of course, it was my first experience in one. We'd start each day around ten, taking a lap around the field, and then doing fifteen minutes of exercises in right field, led by Ellie Howard. Then we'd break into groups, taking turns on all the fundamentals. As a catcher, I'd spend a lot of the time on the poorly developed back field at Fort Lauderdale Stadium, out of the view of the spectators, but getting my work in.

We'd take our turns at bat, and Houk would sit quietly behind the batting cage, taking it all in. For all the years Ralph managed, I can hardly ever remember him being anywhere but perched on the batting cage. Writers could talk to him there, photographers could shoot him there, coaches could talk to him there, MacPhail or Burke could stop by, but his eyes would never leave the action. He never said much as we stepped in to swing, but we knew he was there.

I got a kick out of handling pitchers like Stottlemyre, Peterson, and Bahnsen in Florida, and it helped boost my confidence. Houk told me at one point, "You'll win more games catching than you ever will hitting." With that advice, I realized the importance of the catching position, and worked even harder at it. In college or in the minor leagues, the hitters change each year, and learning how to pitch to different people might be good for only a few months. But once you're in the big leagues, you can figure that what you learn about hitters could last you for years. It's a catcher's responsibility to know, and I took it seriously. And with Houk, Howard, and Hegan around, all former catchers, it was hard to forget.

A pension disagreement delayed the formal opening of spring training a few days, but didn't affect the non-roster players, so I was ahead of everyone when the exhibition games began, and Houk had me behind the plate in the first game. In fact, I got into each of the first six exhibitions and caught two complete games, and both of them were victories. It was really quite unusual for a non-roster catcher to get into any games at all, but as training camp progressed, I continued to see action, sharing the catching duties with Jake Gibbs and Frank Fernandez. And as the cuts were made, I stayed. Houk insisted that I would be going to Syracuse shortly, but I stayed almost until camp broke. The other non-roster catchers, John Ellis and Charlie Sands, were long gone.

I was surprised that I got as much of a chance to play as I did, but I wasn't surprised that I was able to do a good job. I knew from the experience that if I had a chance to catch in the majors right then, I could do all right. The pitchers are smarter in the big leagues, but they throw the ball over the plate, and they weren't supermen. I could hit my share.

Finally, I was assigned to the minor league camp in nearby Hollywood, Florida, where I rejoined most of my Binghamton teammates from the year before, now wearing the uniforms of the Syracuse Chiefs. Since the International League season doesn't open until a couple of weeks after the major leagues begin, we were still in training when the Yankees got rolling. In fact, we were scheduled to play an exhibition with Richmond early in April when I got a call telling me to fly to Detroit.

Fernandez, the Yankees' number two catcher behind Gibbs, had been called into a weekend army reserve meeting, and I was needed to help out in the bullpen and to be available in case of emergency. The emergency never arose, I didn't get into any games, and, although it was my first taste of the major leagues, it was not very memorable. I can't even recall whom I roomed with.

Then came the long-awaited bad news. Uncle Sam wanted Thurman Munson. Just when I was looking forward to
the season and had put the army out of my mind, my notice
came to begin a four-month hitch. I was assigned to duty as
a clerk in Fort Dix, New Jersey, a decent location, as it
would turn out.

If fans think I look squatty in a baseball uniform, they
should have seen me in an ill-fitting army fatigue uniform.
But to tell you the truth, the army wasn't bad. It was hard
work, but we also had fun, and I met a lot of good guys
there. I didn't get to play anything other than softball, but
because I always played hard to win, the games were good
ones.

Stan Bahnsen, the Yankee pitcher who had won the
Rookie of the Year award the season before, would do weekend duty in Fort Dix at times, and he'd catch me up on what
was going on.

Whenever I'd get a weekend pass, I'd fly up to Syracuse
and play for the Chiefs all weekend. If the Chiefs were on
the road, I'd go to Yankee Stadium and take batting practice. So the location was a blessing, because at least I could
keep in touch with the game. At one point, there was word
that I was going to be transferred to New Orleans, but, fortunately, that never came about.

By August, I was ready to write the season off, just as I
had during my freshman year at Kent State. I had gotten
into seventeen games at Syracuse, giving me a total of
eighty-eight professional games. I had only sixty-four at-
bats on those weekend passes, for a 290 total, including the
year at Binghamton. I felt I was really being set back, but
there was nothing I could do about it.

Frank Fernandez was again assigned to weekend reserve
duty in early August, and I got a call to report to Yankee
Stadium instead of Syracuse. This time, I was actually added to the twenty-five-man roster, and my chances for playing looked promising.

It was a festive weekend, with the annual Old Timers' Day scheduled for Saturday. That was not of much concern to me, of course, and as I arrived on late Friday afternoon at the Stadium, I hopped onto the couch in the players' lounge to try to grab a few hours of needed sleep. Not long after I'd dozed off, Houk came by to wake me up. "Don't get too comfortable—you're going to be playing this time," he said. Well, that was okay with me.

BASE HIT OFF CATFISH

I had thought Ralph might have me playing in both games of the twi-night doubleheader, from what he had said, but I was in the bullpen for the first game. In those days, the Yankees would schedule twi-night doubleheaders regularly, but they proved to be unattractive in terms of attendance, and certainly upset the rhythm of the schedule in terms of playing. Nobody likes doubleheaders, particularly when the first game starts in the tough late afternoon shadows.

The Oakland A's, in town for the weekend, were not yet considered a very strong club, but they were on their way toward that recognition. They had Bando, Campaneris, Jackson, Hunter, Fingers, and Rudi, and anyone who knew talent knew that this was a team to watch. The plain fact was, the Yankees were in fifth place with a 54–56 record on this Friday night, and Oakland was running a handsome second to the Twins. Their colorful uniforms, white shoes, and mule mascot were still considered oddball by major league standards, but in the not too distant future, a lot of teams would be stealing Charlie Finley's "eccentric ideas" and making them the normal part of the game.

I warmed up the relief pitchers during the first game, and with the Yankees trailing 5–3 in the tenth, Ralph had me run in from the bullpen to pinch-hit. But the final out of the game was recorded while I waited in the on-deck circle, and my debut would have to wait.

There are usually about thirty minutes between games. On these Friday night situations, they'd often balance the time to see if the second game could start at 8:00 for television purposes. So I had a little time to go over the Oakland hitters with Al Downing, the second game pitcher, before we went onto the field to warm up.

Reggie Jackson was the most devastating hitter at the time for the A's, and by this weekend, he was looking like a good bet to break Roger Maris' home run record. As it was, he tailed off badly toward the end, and didn't even win the home run title. But he was the talk of the league in 1969, and the man Downing and I were most concerned with.

I had worked a couple of games with Downing the year before, when the Yankees sent him to Binghamton to try to work his arm back in shape. It had to be a little embarrassing for Al to pitch in the Eastern League, after having led the American League in strikeouts just a few seasons before, but he was a man about it, and I respected him for it. The experience of having handled him before helped relax me for my assignment.

We were out in front of the dugout warming up when Bob Sheppard announced the starting lineup for the second game. "Batting eighth, the catcher, number fifteen, Thurman Munson, number fifteen."

I got a nice hand from the crowd, and that made me feel pretty good. The number 15 had been worn for many years by Tom Tresh, but he had been traded to Detroit in June, and I inherited it. It was a nice low number to pick up in the middle of the season.

The Oakland pitcher was Catfish Hunter. He had not yet had a winning season in the majors, but everyone respected him as a control pitcher with good stuff, and he had pitched a perfect game the year before, helping to build his reputation.

He walked me my first time up, and in the fifth inning I grounded out. Meanwhile, Downing was pitching quite well, considering that he hadn't yet hurled a complete game for the season and was still struggling along on the comeback trail.

The score was 0–0 as I came up in the last of the seventh. Catfish got a pitch a little up on me, and I lined a clean single to center. It was my first major league hit. It moved Gene Michael over to third, and I took second on the throw. Ellie Howard, coaching at first, made sure we retrieved the ball to save.

Hunter retired Downing on a short fly ball, but then Horace Clarke lined a two-run single, and we grabbed a 2-0 lead.

Downing set the A's down in the eighth, and in the last of the eighth, I came up with the bases loaded and the infield drawn in. The result was a single to right, two more runs scored, and it was a 5–0 ballgame.

We got through the ninth without any trouble, and that was the way the game ended. It was Downing's first complete game and first shutout of the year, and we had really worked well together. I think he shook me off only two or three times the whole game. For the Yankees, it was the start of a four-game winning streak which gave us a spurt of nine wins in ten games, and lifted us over .500 for the first time since April. I felt I had played a big part in it, and rapidly felt as if I belonged.

I stayed at Gene Michael's house that night, and, as I said, Saturday was Old Timers' Day. I posed for a picture with Gene Woodling, my scout, but watched all the festivities and the game from the bullpen. Mel Stottlemyre beat Chuck Dobson 2–1.

Sunday was a single game, the last day before my weekend pass expired. I was hoping to play, and happy to see my name on the lineup card taped to the dugout wall. Fritz Peterson would be working for us against Lew Krausse of the A's.

Fritz was an unusual pitcher in a lot of ways. To begin with, he was an exceptionally fast worker. I know the fans like that, but I like it too—not because the games get over quickly, but because it's a lot easier on legs when you don't have to crouch so long waiting for the pitch. Give me the quick workers any day.

Fritz also had a huge variety of pitches. It seemed as though every spring he'd come up with a new one. One year he developed a "knuckle curve," which he called "the Thing." I didn't even have enough fingers to signal all of his pitches, and I had to use open palm, or fist, or a touch of my thigh. But he was easy to catch, because he was always around the plate. Fritz had outstanding control.

It was a happy day for me. Fritz was sharp the whole game, and we scored an easy 5–1 victory. But the highlight for me came in the sixth inning, when I hit my first major league home run. It was a shot into the lower left field stands off Krausse, and followed a homer by Bobby Murcer. And if that wasn't enough, Gene Michael followed me and also homered. It was a big day for Kent State.

A lot was made of the three homers in a row after the game, especially since all of our names started with M. It was like a reincarnation of the Mantle-Maris days. My home run ball was retrieved, and I posed for photographers holding it in the clubhouse.

So my weekend resulted in three hits in six at bats, a homer, three runs batted in, two runs scored, and I caught two complete game victories in which only one run was scored.

But, as though my carriage would turn into a pumpkin at midnight, I had to get back to Fort Dix after the game. I remember going to sleep that night wondering if it was really possible that only a few hours ago I was hitting a home run in Yankee Stadium.

The army seemed less and less interesting to me now that I'd gotten my first taste of big league pitching. I could still see Hunter's slider and Krausse's fast ball coming into me. I really longed for the end of August, when my four-month hitch would be up and I'd be able to rejoin the Yankees.

I did play a few more weekends with Syracuse, and ran my season stats for them to twenty-eight games with a .363 average. It gave me ninety-nine minor league games and only 328 at-bats. But I knew just from that weekend that I was ready to put my minor league days behind me.

My reserve duty ended on August 30, but the Yankees had me return to Syracuse, where the Chiefs were involved in the International League playoffs. I caught the first two games against Louisville, but, with the weekend approaching, I was summoned to join the Yankees in Cleveland on September 5. I would never again wear a minor league uniform.

In effect, I became a regular that day. Frank Fernandez was positioned in right field, and I caught both ends of the twi-night doubleheader in big Municipal Stadium, where I had once upon a time leaned over the fence and asked Mike Garcia for an autograph. Needless to say, a big Munson contingent, including a load of Diana's relatives, was in attendance. Stottlemyre pitched the first game, and lost 2–1 to Sam McDowell. It was the first game we'd lost with me behind the plate, but I enjoyed working with Mel.

In the second game, it was Peterson again, and he was locked in a tight pitching duel with Dick Ellsworth. Going into the ninth inning, we held onto a 2–0 lead with two out and Chuck Hinton on first. Ken "Hawk" Harrelson was the hitter, representing the tying run.

Now, Ralph always liked to keep the defense alert, and we had a pickoff play in which Joe Pepitone, playing first, would touch his belt buckle, indicating that I should throw to him.

Well, Hinton took his lead, and Pepi went to his belt. Or

at least he said he did, because either I never saw it or I looked at it and it didn't register. No throw. Again he tried it, and again I failed to get the sign. No throw.

Pepi called time out, waving his arms to get the umpire's attention. He came in almost halfway between first and home and shouted my name. As he was yelling, "Hey, Thurman," he grabbed his buckle with his hand, and pulled the whole elastic belt out about eight inches from his waist.

On the next pitch, I fired to Joe, and we picked Hinton off first to end the game. I'll never forget it.

I played almost every day after that. On the next home stand, I beat Boston with a ninth-inning single off Sparky Lyle before a big Sunday crowd. Besides my twenty-eight games for Syracuse, I got into twenty-six games for the Yankees and batted .256 with one homer and nine runs batted in. It wasn't the kind of average I expected to be proud of, but I was just getting my feet wet, of course, and Ralph kept emphasizing to me that my most important assignment would be to begin learning the hitters from a catching standpoint if I was to become the team's regular in 1970.

Twelve men decided to test my throwing arm in those final weeks, and I threw seven of them out. If you can't handle yourself in that department, word spreads quickly, and you're out of a job in a hurry. It was important to do well in that area, to establish my reputation early, and I accomplished that.

My initiation was complete. I had been tested, and I had passed the test. No one made any secret of the fact that I was to be given the full shot at the starting catching assignment for the following season.

GETTING READY FOR THE BIGGIES

Not everyone can play winter ball. The natives of the Latin American countries where leagues exist are of course eligible, and, in fact, almost required to play. If a big Latin star passed up the winter schedule in his own country, it would be a major incident among the home folks. As for American players, each team is allowed only a certain number, and the spots are generally filled by younger players. Frequently, the major league teams will go to great efforts to get one of their prospects situated on a winter league club, but there are also times when the owners of those teams look for players on their own.

I had no doubt that I wanted to play ball in the winter of 1969-70. The army had cost me a lot of valuable playing time, and I was anxious to make up for it. The Yankees were in full agreement, and it was arranged for me to play for the San Juan team in the Puerto Rican League.

Although I'd heard some cautionary stories from other players about conditions out of the States, the San Juan experience was a really nice one for Diana and me. We lived in a nice place and found the people really friendly, and I

was glad to be playing ball again every day. Diana couldn't
stay the whole season, because she was pregnant with our
first child at the time, but it was almost like a second honeymoon in many ways. Finally, she went home to Canton to
stay with her parents.

Our manager in San Juan was Cot Deal, who had once
served as the Yankees' pitching coach under Johnny
Keane. Lee May was our first baseman, and Sid O'Brien
and Coco Laboy were also in the infield. Jose Cardenal, Joe
Lahoud, and Willie Crawford were teammates, and I also
remember that throughout the league were an endless sup-
ply of really young players—seventeen, eighteen years old.
I can hardly remember any of their names, but I'm sure a
number of them are now playing in the major leagues.

I was also a teammate of Roberto Clemente at San Juan.
You can never begin to appreciate what a national hero he
was to the people of Puerto Rico. There's no way I can draw
a comparison with anyone in America, for I've never seen
anything like it. If Roberto had been the sort to exploit the
popularity, he could have gotten anything he wanted and
more. But he was basically a humble and kind man, as concerned with his people as they were with him. There was
obviously no need for Roberto to play winter ball, for his
financial needs were well met by the Pittsburgh Pirates,
and he was well past the point of needing any seasoning.
But had he passed up the chance to play before his home
town fans, it would have been considered a national tragedy.

I remember that all of us watched Clemente with awe every time he stepped into the batting cage during batting
practice. Ordinarily, no one pays attention to the man in
the cage, but in Roberto's case, not only were we watching
carefully, but everyone in the stands became quiet and ob-
served closely, then cheered every time he connected solidly. I remember studying Roberto, noting that although I
was not in his class, he had a similar approach to the game

in terms of hitting—meeting the ball, going to the opposite field, pulling when you got your pitch, etc. And he watched me, too, and while he never was overbearing in the way of giving advice, he told me that if I ever hit .280 in the majors, I should consider it a bad season. It was a nice compliment.

I hit the ball really well in Puerto Rico, and was pleased to know that my irregular playing time of the previous summer hadn't hurt my timing. I batted .333, which was second in the league, and felt ready to go for 1970. I got back to Canton shortly before spring training and negotiated a contract for myself which was thirty-three percent above the minimum salary, based on the belief that I would be a regular. My salary then, for my rookie season, would be $15,000, and I was proud of it.

Naturally, all eyes were on me as spring training opened for the 1970 season, and I was really glad that I'd played a little the year before. It took a lot of the unknowns away and made me feel comfortable about the daily tasks of getting in shape for the season. Of course, playing winter ball had already put me in good shape, and I hit the ball with authority all through the opening workouts.

At the same time, though, eyes began to turn elsewhere. John Ellis, a big and strong catcher who had played in the Carolina League in 1969, was also hitting the ball well. He was also a right-hand hitter, and had also had a shot with the big club the year before, filling in when the army had taken both myself and Fernandez away. And John had hit an inside-the-park home run in his first game, making him an instant hero.

It helped that he was practically a local boy, coming as he did from New London, Connecticut, which was just a couple hours from Yankee Stadium. And as John began to display some of his power in the early going, he took some of the attention away from me.

Since the Yankees were still determined to make me the

catcher, John was placed at first base, where Ralph could
get an idea of his mobility and range. For a man placed at a
new position, he handled himself well, and as spring training rolled on, he was making it clear that a place in the
lineup would have to be found for him.

The main new faces on the club that spring were Danny
Cater, Curt Blefary, Pete Ward, and Ron Hansen. Cater, a
solid .300 hitter, had come from Oakland in a trade for Al
Downing and Frank Fernandez. Blefary, who had once
been Rookie of the Year while with Baltimore, came to us
from Houston in an even-up trade for Joe Pepitone. Ward
and Hansen were utility men.

The absence of Pepitone from camp contributed to a lot of
Pepitone stories all spring. I never got to know Joe very
well, for I hadn't been a teammate very long, but it seemed
as though everyone spoke warmly of him, always mentioned how good he "could have been." Joe himself realized
that he probably missed out on his full potential, but he had
the ability to enjoy life, and decided that a high priority belonged in that area. I can't stand here and judge the man,
but I can say that he generally enjoyed the friendship of everyone he met, and that's a nice tribute to a guy after he's
been traded.

Blefary, on the other hand, had come a long way on the
strength of his rookie season. He had been traded to Houston for Mike Cuellar, and then to the Yankees for Pepi,
both one-sided deals. Curt told me during spring training
that the Yankees wouldn't win the pennant without his hitting .300, belting thirty homers, and driving in 100 runs.
He was right on both counts—he hit .212 with nine homers
and thirty-seven runs batted in, and we didn't win the pennant.

I can't fault Curt for lacking self-confidence, at least on
the outside. I remember him today as the only player who
didn't like Ralph Houk. It came from that age-old complaint of a player on the way down—he wasn't getting

enough of a chance to play. Had the numbers been better for Curt, he might have had a better case.

Ward and Hansen were welcome additions to the team, and it was generally a team of good people in 1970. We all got along well, and it was a happy year to me.

I had a fine spring, hitting around .360, but Ellis remained the talk of the training camp, and on the last day, he received the James P. Dawson Award (a watch), as the best rookie in spring training. I wasn't even second—that went to Ron Klimkowski, the pitcher. I was third, and wasn't bothered a bit. Big John would be taking a lot of heat off me.

ROOKIE OF THE YEAR

The "experts" always seem to pick last year's winner as a sure bet to win again, so everyone considered the 1970 pennant race a lock for the Baltimore Orioles, with the Yankees an also-ran club.

What was pleasing was that many people were picking me to be Rookie of the Year, and saying that on the strength of that honor I would help lift the club up a few notches in the standings.

Well, one man can't accomplish anything quite that lofty, but what was being said was that, as catcher, I would be in a position to help stabilize the team.

It's frequently said that a contender must be strong up the middle; that is, at catcher, at second and short, and in center field. With me behind the plate and Bobby Murcer in center, many were saying that we were on the way toward being strong up the middle. Unfortunately, they were never quite so kind with our keystone combination, and it was at that point that I began to dislike the way the press could malign a reputation.

Gene Michael, my old friend and our regular shortstop,

was coming off what would prove to be his best major
league season—a .272 average in the assumption of the
regular job, replacing Tresh.

"Stick" was an outstanding shortstop—he had great
range to his left and his right, a strong arm, and the ability
to learn quickly how to play the different hitters. As it developed, his .272 was an unusually high showing for him,
and a mark he didn't again approach. For this reason, the
press always acknowledged his fielding but would always
put down his hitting and make him appear to be a weak
link in the lineup. This simply wasn't the case. Teams have
won pennants with players far worse than Stick, and if the
rest of the lineup is hitting as it should, people needn't look
to offensive productivity from the shortstop.

Nevertheless, Gene was a charmer, and became a popular player in New York. He was bright and witty and made
friends with a lot of the writers. So they were never as cruel
to him as they were to Horace Clarke.

Horace, our second baseman, was a polite gentleman
from the Virgin Islands, who bothered no one and never
sought to answer critics with his mouth. He lived a simple
life, was devoted to his family, and went about his business
in a quiet way. He was the last Yankee to ever live in the
Yankee Stadium neighborhood, sacrificing more luxurious
surroundings for the simple convenience of walking to
work. And Horace never made a lot of money, so I'm sure
there were financial considerations.

As a player, Horace was as durable as they came. Every
year, he'd give you 150–160 games, a remarkable accomplishment in view of the difficulties of the schedule. He'd
play them all—two in one day, day games after night
games, twi-night doubleheaders, all the exhibitions. Now,
he wasn't the world's greatest defensive player, but the
durability helped him set a record for consecutive seasons
leading the league in assists, a record held by Hall of Famer Charlie Gehringer.

Yes, there may have been times when Horace didn't hang in as long as he should have on double plays. And maybe his range left a little to be desired. But he was by no means a casualty out there. He led the league in double plays a few times, made his share of great catches, and very seldom committed an error on fundamentals.

As an offensive player, he would give you more than most second basemen. Every year, he'd have about 180 hits. He'd move the runners and bunt well. He was a terrific base stealer, finishing among the all-time Yankee leaders. As a leadoff man, he didn't walk as much as he might have, but he got on base a lot. He led the league in at bats three times.

But at second he was succeeding Bobby Richardson, a very popular Yankee from the championship years, and the fans could never warm up to this man. Their disenchantment was fanned by a hostile New York press, who maligned him repeatedly and tended to label all the post-pennant years as the Horace Clarke Era. In fact, Horace was one of the better players the Yankees produced in that period, and it certainly wasn't his fault that the team couldn't develop a better second baseman.

The writers would have a field day at Horace's expense, and Horace would never answer them. He'd pretend to not even see what they were writing, but we knew he had to be aware of it, and it used to bother his wife a lot. He was close friends with Roy White, who also took his share of abuse, and he'd confide to Roy now and then that the publicity was a source of embarrassment to him.

What never came out was that Horace never even made $40,000 a year in salary—not even after seventeen years in the Yankee organization and ten in the majors as a regular. If he was an unusually high-paid man, then the people could be perhaps a bit more justified in occasional criticism. But he gave the club more than their money's worth for a long time, and when he was finally sold to San Diego in

1974, he left without anyone even bothering to say thank you for seventeen years.

Horace, a private man, was not the sort to keep in touch, and I have no idea what he's doing today back home in the Virgin Islands. But I hope he's making some good money and enjoying the beautiful Islands, sitting back with a fishing rod, and thinking out loud with a chuckle, "I wonder how all my old friends on the press are doing these days."

The season opened in Yankee Stadium on April 7 with a small opening-day crowd of less than 22,000 to see the Red Sox. I was the catcher, but all the attention was on John Ellis, who was playing first and batting cleanup. Mrs. Lou Gehrig had sent him a letter before the game, saying something to the effect of "I've waited all these years for Lou's successor, and now he's here."

Gary Peters beat us 4–3, and I was hitless. But against Ray Culp two days later, I got a hit, as Fritz beat Boston 4–3, and I felt things were looking good thus far. I knew I wasn't swinging the bat as well as I was capable of doing, but I didn't give any thought to a slump.

On Friday night, the 10th, my first baby was born. Diana gave birth to six-pound fourteen-ounce Tracy Lynn Munson at Timken Mercy Hospital in Canton. It was pass-out-cigar time in New York, but my thoughts were with Diana and the baby, and I regretted not being there with them.

Although my mind was in Canton, I was still very much thinking baseball as the Indians came to town for a weekend series. We lost two of the three games, and I didn't get a single hit. I don't think it had anything to do with Diana, but I was beginning to get bothered by it.

Right after the doubleheader on Sunday, I caught a flight home to see my baby. It's a great feeling to see your firstborn for the first time. I was about the happiest I'd ever been—really the proud papa.

We didn't play again until Tuesday night in Boston, so I had a nice visit with the family before rejoining the club.

But things didn't improve at Fenway Park, as we lost three straight before an eleven-inning victory, and I still couldn't buy a hit.

Ellis wasn't doing much more than I was, and that was taking some of the heat off me, but I was really beside myself now. If the team had been winning, it might have been easier, but my bad start was directly tied to the team's losing, and I felt a big share of that responsibility.

We went to Baltimore for three games, and lost two of them. We were 4-8 for the season, and you guessed it, I still had the one hit. I was one for thirty, and hadn't had a hit in my last twenty-four at-bats.

Outwardly, I remained confident. "I'll still hit three hundred," I told people, not quite sure of myself.

I'd had slumps before, but this was my first real initiation into the majors. Could it be I wasn't ready? Were ninety-nine minor league games not enough? Had I arrived at a level of play I couldn't handle?

I really didn't believe that, but I did have some sleepless nights. Finally, Ralph called me into his office. He knew I was concerned.

"Thurman," he said, "I told you you'd win more games for this club catching than you would hitting. You've just got to relax. You're my regular catcher, and no one is sending you down or sitting you down. Just get out there and play the way I know you can."

It did relax me, and it let me know that Ralph was aware of my concerns, even without my having confided in him. We went to Washington on Monday night, the 20th, to face George Brunet. And don't you know, I had three hits, including a double, and drove in two runs as we beat the Senators 11–2. The next night, Ralph sat me down.

"I just wanted you to think about those three hits a little longer," he said. "Otherwise, you might go hitless tonight and start worrying all over again."

I didn't have another slump the rest of the season.

We were only 9–12, in April, but we won seven of eight to start the month of May, and things were beginning to jell for us. Peterson and Stottlemyre were pitching quite well, and Stan Bahnsen was doing a good job. The bullpen was developing as our big story, with Lindy McDaniel, Jack Aker, and Steve Hamilton doing great work for us.

McDaniel was an interesting guy, and certainly not your routine ballplayer. As a lay preacher in the Church of Christ, he seemed concerned with converting us all. Some guys resented his monthly mailing of "Pitching for the Master," but most guys, like myself, simply ignored it, thinking, "Lindy's just doing his thing." As I recall, he did win over a couple of converts that year—a batboy and an outfielder—so I'm sure he considered his season to be a good one.

On the mound, which was where my real interest was, he was super. His forkball was breaking all over the place, and he was a great competitor. He saved twenty-nine and won nine for us in 1970 with a 2.01 ERA, and was one of the main reasons for our successful year.

Hamilton and Aker were sort of "mature veterans," both above the shenanigans of us younger players, but both respected as among the brighter members of the team, and, for 1970, among the most successful.

Hamilton was our player representative, and managed to remain close to both Lee MacPhail, and Marvin Miller, director of the Players' Association. Aker later became the rep, so you can see that both were of a distinguished class. Except for the period when Bobby Murcer had the job, we always took the election very seriously and looked to the office for answers to a whole host of questions. Hamilton and Aker were the best we had, and Aker had the difficult responsibility of serving in the post during the strike a few years later.

I batted second a good deal of the year, an unusual spot for a catcher, but I did have good speed, particularly for one

built as stockily as I was. The pitching was being comple-
mented by the hitting, with Cater, White, myself, Ron
Hansen, Jake Gibbs, Frank Tepedino, and Jim Lyttle all
flirting with the .300 mark.

Gibbs, the man I succeeded, was having a particularly
productive year for part-time play. He got into only forty-
nine games that year, but he hit eight homers and drove in
twenty-six runs. He was also great to me, seeing as how I'd
taken his job away. But Jake, who had signed as a third
baseman in the first place, was a classy guy, who handled
his new responsibilities in a professional way. When he retired the following year, there was a Jake Gibbs Day at
Yankee Stadium, and not too many players with Jake's credentials had ever been so honored.

At the All-Star break, we were 46-39, seven games behind the Orioles, and playing well. I didn't make the All-
Star team, which was fine with me, for it gave me more
time to spend with the baby. And I was determined to have
a big second half.

We started out winning three of four from Oakland after
the break, and by August 1 had moved into second place.
Just as we were rolling, my two weeks of reserve duty came
up, and off I went to Fort Dix, leaving the Yankees behind
me. One game that really stands in my mind, though, just
preceded the two-week hitch.

I was doing weekend duty, and the Yankees were playing
Baltimore at home. Sunday was a doubleheader, and it was
doubtful that I could get to the park in time for even the
second game. But I drove like crazy and got to the clubhouse halfway through the nightcap.

No one really knew I had arrived, and the Yankees were
locked in a close game in this big series. I dressed and headed for the dugout, and not long after I got there, Ralph said,
"Grab a bat and pinch-hit."

I walked to the on-deck circle, and the fans near the dugout began to cheer. Then it spread from section to section,

and soon the whole crowd of some 42,000 was on its feet, giving me a standing ovation as my name was announced.

I'm sure the element of surprise had a great deal to do with it, and the roar of the crowd was deafening. It was as though, at that very moment, I had become appreciated by the New York fans. I had, in a sense, arrived.

Pete Richert was pitching, and I fouled off about seven pitches before I lined hard to Brooks Robinson for an out. We lost the game in eleven innings and fell nine and a half games out of first, but I couldn't help feeling satisfied with myself as I drove home.

With Baltimore's big lead, there was not much of a pennant race, so we played out the rest of the schedule looking to hold onto second place while reaching personal achievements. I was really stinging the ball, and batted .348 after the All-Star break. We didn't have much power, with only Murcer and White reaching double figures in home runs, but we were scoring enough runs to keep winning. We won ninety-three games, two of which were particularly memorable.

The first was the game in which we clinched second place. Despite a team lacking big names and great stars, we had really had a helluva season. And we were a close team, too. So Ralph decided that we would celebrate the clinching with a champagne party in the clubhouse. Looking back on it now, I find it a little ridiculous. We were whooping it up as though we'd won the pennant. I know old Yankee purists must have thought that celebrating second place was really bush, but we enjoyed it, and to tell the truth, it was more fun than when we won the pennant six years later, if only because there were no TV cameras and no mob of strange people clawing their way into the clubhouse. It was our party, and we enjoyed it.

Then, in the final game of the year, Fritz Peterson went after his twentieth victory. It was a tough assignment, since we were playing in Fenway Park, a difficult park for any left-hander. And Fritz wanted the twentieth so badly he could taste it. He even changed his hotel room, which was originally 1219, because, he explained, "If I lose, my record will be 19–12, which is the reverse of 1219."

Fritz was one of the most fun-loving guys you could ever meet. He would always be ordering magazine subscriptions in Stottlemyre's name or thinking up elaborate practical jokes to pull. He was the king when it came to dreaming up nicknames, and he'd buy almost anything on a whim if it looked halfway interesting in the airline magazines.

He would have liked to pitch a complete game in Boston, but he'd take the win any way he could get it. We had a 4–3 lead in the ninth when Ralph decided to bring McDaniel in.

Fritz couldn't bear to watch his fate in someone else's hands. He couldn't stay in the dugout and watch, and when he went into the clubhouse, the game was on the radio. To escape from the pressure, he went into Ralph's office, crouched under Ralph's desk, and held his hands over his ears. Not until the game was over and everyone piled into the clubhouse did he come out and say, "Who won?"

Fritz had won his twentieth. What a character!

I played 132 games that year and, true to my prediction, batted .302, tops on the club. I had six homers and fifty-three runs batted in, hitting second most of the year, and caught forty of sixty-nine runners trying to steal. I led the league with eighty assists, which can be a little misleading, because a catcher gets an assist if he drops a third strike and has to throw his man out at first. Not that that happened a lot, but I just mention it to point out that statistics can sometimes be misleading.

There would be no winter ball for me this time. I was looking forward to getting home, where Diana and I were building a new house, and to just relax. I planned to spend the off-season playing golf and working out at the YMCA. I had never played that many games in one season before, and really felt like I could use the rest.

The Rookie of the Year voting was announced in November. I got twenty-three out of twenty-four possible votes, with the other vote going to Cleveland outfielder Roy Foster.

Being Rookie of the Year was a nice honor, and I was the first catcher ever so named in the American League. The only other catcher in the majors had been Johnny Bench. Those things were what made the honor gather significance for me, not the fact that I beat out a handful of guys to win. But the accomplishment meant a lot to me in terms of my being spoken of in the same breath as Bench.

Ralph was the Manager of the Year for bringing home the team with ninety-three victories, and so the year had been even better than predicted all around.

AN UNSATISFYING
FOLLOWUP

One of the many clichés we all live with in baseball is the "sophomore jinx," the so-called malady that affects anyone in his second season following a good rookie year. I really got tired of having writers and announcers ask me about it in spring training in 1971, because it was ridiculous, and just a dumb question. I had never had any sort of jinx in my life. They're all mental anyway, and I wasn't having any problem with my confidence.

Coming off the good season, both mine and the club's, we were all expected to do great things. I figured that I could only be better in '71, with the added experience of knowing the opposing hitters better and knowing our own pitchers better.

But after the first week of the season, I couldn't believe what was happening. It was the same horrible start all over again that I had experienced in 1970. I was two for thirty, including an 0-for-twenty-seven slump, and I was hitting .067. The team was playing .500, but I wasn't contributing a thing. And I got nervous about it. I started changing my stance and experimenting, and I lost my confidence at the plate. Ralph kept saying, "Don't worry, you started like this last year and hit three hundred." But all the preseason talk of a sophomore jinx was starting to haunt me. And my weekend military obligations, once a month, were no help, either. Just as I'd start to hit, off I'd go and miss three or four games. I was lifting my average slowly, but nothing like the previous year, and I just couldn't catch fire at the plate.

Fortunately, the slump at the plate didn't affect my catching. If I couldn't contribute at bat, I sure wasn't going to let my whole game fall apart. The Yankees had doubled my salary after my rookie season, and I was determined that they were going to get their $30,000 worth one way or another.

My reputation for throwing runners out was never stronger than it was in 1971. For the entire season, only thirty-eight men tried to steal on me, and I nailed twenty-three of them. The mark of a good catcher is not so much how many you catch stealing as how many don't even try to steal out of respect for your arm.

On June 18, we were playing a night game in Baltimore before some 40,000 fans—a sensational crowd for that city. Mike Cuellar was pitching against Fritz Peterson, and we were trying to cut into the Orioles' lead before the season got away from us. The Orioles were in first, and we were fourth, eleven games out, and needed some quick victories.

Midway through the game, one of those unavoidable situations arose that goes down as an occupational hazard for catchers. It was a routine hit to the outfield, and here came the Orioles' Andy Etchebarren heading for home. I moved up the line and took the throw, and then the three of us—I, Andy, and the ball—crashed together at once. I dropped the ball, Andy tumbled over the plate, and I blacked out. The impact was fierce, and the result was a run scored.

I was taken to the hospital, where I was examined by a neurosurgeon and pronounced okay. Reading about it in the papers the next day, I noted that I'd been charged with an error for dropping the ball, which is just one of those things. The irony of the play, it developed, was that the error was the only one charged to me all season. I handled 614 other chances successfully, and the fielding percentage of .998 tied the all-time Yankee record for catchers, held by Ellie Howard. And only one man in major league history—Buddy Rosar of the 1946 Athletics—had ever fielded 1.000 behind the plate for a full season. So I just missed out on a major league record by being knocked unconscious.

It was not a bad play by Etchebarren, and we still kid about it to this day. A catcher is no more cautious about knocking over his opposite number than another player would be, and it was a clean play. I didn't play it as I should have, but I was still learning some of the finer points of the game. A few weeks earlier, I hadn't properly slid into Duane Josephson in Boston, and it had cost us a run. But a few weeks later, by the oddest of coincidences, I had occasion to run into Etchebarren at the plate, and I scored a run. So you learn by experience, even if it's sometimes painful.

Baltimore manager Earl Weaver named me to the All-Star team for 1971, the first time I was ever selected. Ray Fosse had been voted the starting catcher by the fans, but he was injured, and Bill Freehan of Detroit started. The game was played in Detroit, and Murcer and I were the only Yankee representatives. I got into the game in the last two innings to catch Mickey Lolich, and the American League won 6–4. It was the only American League victory in years, and I'm proud to have participated in it.

I remember Johnny Bench coming to bat, and just asking me how I was. I'm usually the one chatting all the time behind the plate, but I was pretty nervous in that game, and Bench must have sensed it. "Why am I so nervous?" I said to Johnny. He kind of laughed and said, "Because you're supposed to be."

Bench is one of the really classy people I've met in the game. It's a real honor to be compared to him, and frankly, it doesn't bother me at all if people rate me second to him. I'm nowhere near the power hitter that he is, and he's had some remarkable seasons. He's also an athlete to be much admired. He's got a good business sense, and always the ability to say or do the right thing.

On the field, they sometimes talk about Johnny's never having hit .300. But let me tell you, this is a Hall of Famer for sure, because he contributes to a team in so many ways, not the least of it in leadership.

Johnny was married briefly a few years ago, and after all the publicity that surrounded his wedding, it was somewhat embarrassing when it all ended in a year. I didn't speak to him about that, because I just don't know him that well, but when we played the Reds in spring training shortly after the separation, everyone was sort of kidding him about it. I know it had to be a little embarrassing, as well as rather personal, but Johnny handled it very well, and showed the ability to deal with personal problems that celebrities are forced to open to the public.

The only unkind comments I heard Johnny use were directed toward a New York newspaperman who had stopped just short of libel in suggesting some outrageous things about his marriage. What else is new?

Carlton Fisk, on the other hand, has long been compared to me, and without just cause. He came up in late 1971, won the Rookie of the Year Award in '72, ("the only catcher besides Thurman Munson . . . "), and had the benefit of playing in Fenway Park, a place perfectly suited to his swing. I was playing in Yankee Stadium, with its frustrating Death Valley dimensions in left field, and still putting together good seasons.

The press has always made a big thing of the so called rivalry between Fisk and myself, and probably they have exaggerated. While we don't exchange Christmas cards, we're not hostile toward each other. We exchange greetings when one or the other comes to bat, and undoubtedly the "rivalry" is enhanced by the fact that we play for such arch rivals as New York and Boston. If we played for Seattle and Minnesota, who'd care, right?

The only thing that really bothers me about the Fisk-Munson comparisons is that Fisk has never really done the things I've done over a full season. He gets hurt so much that his statistics are often only a partial indication of his ability. He is a good player, but a catcher has got to be durable to be valuable. He never demonstrated strength in that area until 1977.

I think Curt Gowdy had a lot to do with Fisk's popularity. He used to broadcast the Game of the Week and was always building up the Red Sox, the team he used to work for and probably still rooted for. Fisk, big and handsome, became a hero to Gowdy and, in turn, a media hero to America. I don't fault the fans for being caught up in Fisk's media blitz, but I think the records speak for themselves, and naturally, it's upsetting when he scores so much better than I do in the All-Star game elections.

If Fisk handled the so-called feud with more class, I'd respect him more for it. In fact, the two of us could enjoy some laughs over it, watching the fans and the press overreact. But Fisk gets caught up in it, too, and at times goes out of his way to add fuel to the fire by using the press to put me or the Yankees down. Only once did I ever bring it up to him. It was in spring training in 1977, after he'd said some unnecessary things about myself and Reggie Jackson in the papers. When we played the Red Sox and I saw him, I said, "Fisk, I just want you to know one thing. I never said anything bad about you."

People ask me if it bothers me that Fisk gets television commercials. After all, New York is supposed to be the media capital of the world. They say, "If you're a star in New York, that's where the opportunity is."

That's not at all true, and it doesn't bother me anyway. Think back over the last decade, of all the great players in New York—Tom Seaver, Joe Namath, Walt Frazier, Willis Reed, Earl Monroe, Mel Stottlemyre, Bobby Murcer, Rod Gilbert. Outside of Namath and Seaver, how much have they really done? After all, there's only so much to go around, and it doesn't get spread out that much.

Meanwhile, my troubles in the 1971 season continued. Not only was I making mechanical errors that I hadn't made in 1970, but a lot was going on off the field. Besides my bothersome military interruptions, my mother suffered a stroke near the end of the summer, and that was much on my mind.

When Diana became pregnant with our second child, it was a difficult pregnancy, and that was a source of worry. We were still having a house built in Canton, and my mind was a million places at once. I'd fly home on every available off day, and there were a lot of times I just felt like giving up.

The team settled into fourth place on July 2 and never left it. We stayed around the .500 mark all season, and in fact were on the verge of an 81-81 season when we were trailing the Senators in Washington on the final night of the year. It was also the final game ever played in the nation's capital, and the fans were in a hostile mood, threatening to interrupt play all night. We were losing when they finally poured onto the field in what seemed like utter frustration, and the umpires and police were helpless in restoring order. We were awarded a forfeit victory, and the season ended with our record 82-80.

I played only 125 games, thanks to all the army reserve meetings, and I wound up hitting just .251 with ten homers and forty-two runs batted in. It was a most unsatisfying season, despite my fielding record, and I was glad to put it behind me.

BUILDING TOWARDS
A FUTURE

Our second daughter, Kelly, was born on December 20, 1971. She was a beautiful Christmas present for Diana and me, and also for Tracy, who was old enough to enjoy a playmate. With two children, I was now feeling more than ever the joy of parenthood, and there was no doubt in my mind that my family was the most important thing in my life.

Their security became foremost in my thoughts, and my continued development both in baseball and in business seemed perfectly suited toward attaining all I wanted for them.

My friendships and business contacts were moving me toward rapid growth financially, and I was living much better than most people who were earning just $30,000 a year, as I was. It was fortunate for me that I was getting good guidance, and also that I was quick to learn, because ultimately a successful businessman must be responsible for his own actions, and mustn't become overdependent on the advice of others.

People have been eager to enter into partnership with me in various real estate deals, often out of their own insecurity in the field as much as a lack of finances. But partnerships can become a burden, and the pride of driving by a shopping center or an apartment complex and being able to say "*I* own that," is a source of much satisfaction to me.

Players were already starting to kid me about owning half the state of Ohio, and I was proud of being respected as more than an athlete. My business sense was still developing, and my land holdings weren't overwhelming, but I was getting better and better at it all the time, and the combination of family, baseball, and business was making me very happy with life.

The talk of the winter, as far as the Yankees were concerned, was the trading of Stan Bahnsen to Chicago for Rich McKinney. It was an even-up trade, with the Yankees feeling an excess of starting pitchers and the need for a third baseman. I had liked Bahnsen a great deal, and in some ways, this was the first trade that I felt involved a friendship. In fact, Stan and I became even closer after the trade, keeping in touch whenever possible. We had worked well together as a battery, and, speaking personally, I thought the trade seemed odd.

I wasn't alone in my thinking—the majority of fans also questioned it. McKinney was a rather untested product who had hit well against the Yankees in 1971. The reaction seemed to be not so much that McKinney would fail, but that Bahnsen could have brought more. In fairness, most people thought Jim Fregosi was the man to get, and when the Mets got him, that turned out to be a poor deal, too. So you can never tell.

I signed my 1972 contract for $37,500 on the first day of spring training, and that was the first chance I had to really meet McKinney. From the start, we had doubts about him. He quickly picked up a couple of nicknames among us—"Orbit," because he seemed so spaced out, and "Bozo" because his curly hair really poked out from under his cap.

The trade was doomed early. McKinney couldn't make it

at third base or at bat, and he was off to Syracuse before we
knew it. It was just a miserable trade, and really set us
back in an attempt to strengthen ourselves. And Lee Mac-
Phail, who made it, never alibied for it. He'd be the first to
say that it was one of his worst.

Toward the end of spring training, though, Lee swung
one of his better ones. He traded Danny Cater even up to
the Boston Red Sox for Sparky Lyle.

Cater, a .300 hitter, was not a big run producer, and had
little speed and only a fair glove. We liked him and were
sorry to see him go, but we were really enthusiastic about
Lyle.

The bullpen in 1971 had been a dismal failure, account-
ing for a dozen saves combined all season. In Lyle, we were
picking up one of the top relief pitchers in baseball and a
terrific guy to have on the team. I can't remember ever seeing Ralph as happy as he was the day we completed that
deal.

Lyle was not the easiest man to catch, even though he
was basically a one-pitch pitcher. He threw this hard slider
about ninety-five percent of the time, and it comes in on hitters and really intimidates them. But he was in the dirt a
lot, as McDaniel had frequently been, and a catcher could
get a lot of bruises working with either of them.

Intimidation was Sparky's game, and he was a master at
it. As success followed success, he'd get even more dramatic. He was at his peak, theatrically, in 1972, when he'd
come into a game in the bullpen car, to the organist's
strains of "Pomp and Circumstance" played quite regally.
He'd jump out of the car with a big chaw of tobacco in his
cheek, throw his jacket at the batboy, storm to the mound,
and fire his warmups. Then he'd stand there, staring at the
hitters, almost daring them to hit his hard slider.

After that season, he wanted the organist to stop playing
the music, because it was building a little more pressure on
him than he really needed. But everything else about his
act remained intact.

I like Sparky Lyle's attitude on the mound. If you win, you win; if you don't, you don't. Sparky can give up a tenth-inning home run and just walk off the mound with his head high—he knows he'll get them next time.

Even during the most tense situations, Sparky maintains his confidence and his humor on the mound. I remember one game in which he relieved. When he got to the mound, I reminded him the bases were loaded, and there was no place to put anyone.

Still, he threw three consecutive balls, so I went out to the mound again to slow him down. For lack of anything better to say, I again reminded him that the bases were loaded and we couldn't walk anyone.

Sparky looked suddenly at third, at second, and at first, noticed runners everywhere, and said to me, "I thought you were kidding!"

He struck out the batter.

Another time, he came into a game with three men on, and I called for his best (and frequently only) pitch, his slider. The first pitch was hard enough, but it seemed to back up. I didn't notice any break to it.

He threw another pitch, also a ball, and again no break. Then came a third pitch, again after I called for a slider, and he hit the batter. I realized that he hadn't been throwing sliders at all, but plain old fastballs. Out I went to the mound.

"What's going on here?" I said. "What happened to the sliders?"

"Oh, I didn't like the way the game was going," he said.

I admire Sparky's happy-go-lucky approach to life. There are times I wish I could be more carefree and do the oddball things he does for a good time. He's really a free spirit. Who knows—without his hard slider, he'd probably be driving a truck in Pennsylvania and enjoying life just as much.

On a few occasions in 1972, Lyle came into a game in the ninth inning with the game on the line, the bases loaded, and no one out. He seemed to thrive on the pressure situations, and if he'd get through them, he'd really give the team a lift. I remember his doing it against Texas, when all three hitters were right-handed, and again against Detroit in August, when he struck out all three men. The crowd and the players were so up that in his exuberance Sparky fired the ball into the upper deck after I'd thrown it back to him following the final strike. Few games in those early years were as exciting to us.

Murcer hit thirty-three home runs for us that year, and although no one else was having a big season, we made a nice pennant race out of it.

The season started, to everyone's shock, with a players' strike that canceled the first seven games. When play resumed, many fans were saying, "That's it, I'll never watch another game again, that's the final straw." Today, the strike is a distant memory, and the game is healthier than ever. No one likes a strike, and it caught many of the players by surprise, too, but it was good in that it established the strength of the player's union and made us an equal force in future negotiations with management.

The season was very close, with Baltimore, Detroit, and Boston all sharing the top spot at one time or another. And although we never made it to first place, we were never more than eight games from the top. And after the All-Star Game, we really began to move.

We were doing it, as I said, without any big stars, and it reminded me a great deal of my rookie season, when Houk had the team rolling, and we'd look around to try to figure out who was making it roll.

Sparky was, of course, the main man. Steve Kline was having a fine year as a starting pitcher, with Peterson and Stottlemyre contributing. The key to our staying in the race, though, seemed to be in the fourth starter. In the first half of the year, Mike Kekich had the assignment, and he won ten games before beginning to struggle. His place was taken by Rob Gardner, a veteran of many minor league seasons, who was given a chance to pitch, and responded with eight big victories. So we got eighteen wins out of our number four spot in the rotation, and that kept us flying.

Murcer had his thirty-three homers, but his average fell almost forty points. Roy White was a steady outfielder who got on base a lot, but he hit cleanup much of the year and drove in only fifty-four runs. Horace was hitting only .241 and Stick .233. After McKinney failed, we got a lift out of a Mexican League player, Celerino Sanchez, who had a rifle for an arm, and became a real favorite of the fans.

Veteran Felipe Alou played his heart out for us, and Ron Blomberg hit fourteen homers in only 300 at bats, playing only against right-handers. And although I was having a better year than the previous one, I would hit only .280, with seven homers and forty-six runs batted in. I knew I was capable of more.

Still, we'd go out every day and hold our own. Billy Martin had his Detroit Tigers playing good ball with a veteran club, but he couldn't pull away. We were in third place at the end of July, but only six and a half games out of first. We went to Boston to open August, split four games, but gained a game and a half to move within five. Then we took three out of four in Milwaukee and cut the lead to four.

We took a one-day break and went to Cooperstown for the annual Hall of Fame Game, and Bernie Allen hit three homers to give us an 8–3 win over the Dodgers. I played left field that day, my first departure from catching since I'd joined the Yankees. As I would later prove, no matter how good an athlete you are, you've got to stay with a position to play it well. No position is easy if you're not used to it. I played a few games in the outfield in 1976 and really embarrassed myself. I played a little at third and first, too, and fortunately didn't have a chance to make a fool of myself.

We got home for a big series with Detroit, and, in many ways, it was the first big series the Yankees had played in since their last pennant in 1964.

By Thursday night, we had taken two out of three, and
39,000 fans showed up to see Steve Kline battle Joe Cole-
man. It was pennant fever in New York. That was the game
in which Lyle came into the game in the ninth, struck out
the side, and preserved a 1–0 victory. It put us two behind
Detroit, and one and a half behind Baltimore, and it was
time for the front office to start thinking about a World Series.

Milwaukee came to town, and we took three out of four.

We went on the road and got swept in Kansas City, but
lost only half a game in the standings. From there on, we
just stayed close, winning a few, losing one, winning some
more, losing a couple, no big streaks either way. Anyone
could have blown the race open with just a five- or six-game
winning streak, but it didn't come—not for the Tigers, the
Orioles, or the Yankees. And even Boston was beginning to
enter the race.

By the end of August, we were still third, one and a half
behind Baltimore and one behind Detroit, who had fallen to
second.

We still didn't know what was keeping us up, but there's
nothing as exciting as a pennant race in September, with
everyone playing every day. If you don't think players steal
glances at the scoreboards to see how the other clubs are doing, you're wrong. In fact, the old Yankee Stadium scoreboard had permanent out-of-town scores, and the new one,
which cost about $3 million, doesn't. That's an improve-
ment?

We were a gutsy crew, those '72 Yankees, and stayed hot
for a few more weeks before finally dropping out of the
race. We wound up losing five straight to end the season,
and didn't even finish in the money, getting a second
straight fourth-place finish. It was a sudden and very disappointing finish.

I was just a few months old and Harry Truman was president when I posed for my first formal baby portrait in 1947.

My mom claims that this is the earliest photo of me in a baseball uniform. I was nine at the time and playing Little League ball in Canton, Ohio.

After my freshman year in high school I gained weight and my body took its current shape. I was captain of the Lehman High basketball team.

Above: This was the Munson form at Kent State, were I earned All-America honors, something I still rank as high as my Most Valuable Player Award. Tapered uniform pants hadn't yet made their way to Ohio in the late '60's. *(Kent State photo) Right:* I was captain of the Lehman football team, giving me a year-round sports schedule. I had some football scholarship offers, but I decided to play baseball at Kent State. *Below:* I'm number 19, about to catch a pass for Lehman. Football was big in Ohio, and we even played night games.

My first season in pro ball was 1968. I played for Binghamton, New York, and would have led the league in hitting if I'd had a few more times at bat.

Binghamton played an exhibition game in Yankee Stadium in 1968— my first trip to New York. You can see how we packed the stands for the game. This was my first time at bat in Yankee Stadium. *(Louis Requena)*

The man on the right, presenting me with an award, is Gene Woodling, the Yankee scout who watched me play at Kent State. Gene went weeks without saying a word to me before he finally introduced himself.

I married Diana Dominick right after the 1968 season, in Canton. We'd known each other since grade school. *(Ricci Studio)*

An interview after a game in 1969. Already I look cautious about answering questions from the press.

I hit my first major league home run on August 10, 1969, and the ball was retrieved so I could save it.

Watching batting practice as a rookie. I had a lot to learn about the major leagues, and I was in a hurry to learn everything I could.

They teach you respect when you're a rookie. Here I was felled by a pitch, and Dick Howser, Bobby Murcer, Elston Howard and Ralph Houk check me out.

I was voted American League Rookie of the Year for 1970. Here I am receiving the award the following season from former winners Curt Blefary, Dick Howser, and Ron Hansen.

The blue racing past me at the plate is Kansas City's Lou Piniella, later a teammate. It you're in the league long enough, you never know who will be playing with you the next season.

A complete game victory is a source of great satisfaction to both catcher and pitcher, as Stan Bahnsen and I show here in 1971.

This sequence, with me as the runner and the Angels' John Stephenson catching, illustrates the impact on plays at the plate.

It hurts just as much on either end. *(Louis Requena)*

Bobby Murcer and I remain good friends, and we still talk on the phone during the season. His trade to the Giants in 1974 shocked a lot of people, including Bobby.

I don't get to see Johnny Bench very often, but he's a man I really admire, and I'm proud when people compare me to him. This photo is from spring training in 1972.

"I'LL STICK TO BUILDING SHIPS"

The off-season between 1972 and 1973 was an eventful one, of least importance being my decision to grow a mustache. The whole world was turning hippie, so why shouldn't I? Actually, I welcomed the chance to grow one, now that they were more fashionable in baseball, and when I let it droop on the sides a bit, I became well identified by the stache.

"Let this walrus off at Sea World," Lou Piniella once told a bus driver as we got on a team bus together. I suppose the mustache did make me a bit gruff-looking, but I liked it, and that was all that mattered.

In November, the Yankees swung a big trade with Cleveland which brought Graig Nettles to New York. The trade cost us John Ellis, a good friend, along with Jerry Kenney, Rusty Torres, and Charlie Spikes. Spikes was the guy Cleveland wanted most, as he figured to become a fine outfielder, but in getting Nettles, we got one of the best third baseman in the game. He was a guy, like Lyle the year before, we had been hoping to get for some time, and I was delighted when I heard about the trade.

Aside from wearing the same uniform number, nine, Graig and an earlier Yankee, Roger Maris, are very similar. While I've never met Maris, I've certainly heard a lot about him. They apparently have a similar disposition, which can be misinterpreted by the press as surly but is in fact warm and friendly.

Acquiring Nettles, who became the first Yankee since Maris to lead the league in home runs, was a major step toward building a winning ball club. He has been an anchor to the team at third, where he has developed into one of the greatest defensive players I've ever seen, ranking in my mind with Paul Blair, a great outfielder. And I'm not forgetting Brooks Robinson, who was super.

Graig is not only amazingly durable, never missing more than a couple of games a year, but he's got such great patience. It seems as though every year he starts out hitting a hundred and a half before he gets his bat going in the summer. And yet he doesn't let it get to him. He plays as spectacularly as ever at third base and doesn't press at the plate. He knows the hits will come.

It was funny that the one year he didn't start off poorly at the plate, 1974, he hit eleven home runs in April to tie a major league record. What a beauty!

Graig is one of those guys you really have to get to know. Unlike, say, Whitey Ford, he's not your friend the minute he meets you. People think he's aloof, and maybe a bit sour, but those of us who have been his teammates have come to like him a great deal. He's got a good wit, good intelligence, and a good heart. It's funny, though, that he's considered to be almost a carbon copy of Roger Maris in terms of public portrayal and how those who know him see him. Nettles and Maris both wore number nine, both came to the Yankees in major trades, and both led the league in home runs. I think, however, that if Nettles had to go through the kind of pressure Maris had to he'd handle it pretty well. Oh, he wouldn't get along with the newspapermen any better, but it wouldn't bother him once he left the ball park.

The off-season shock waves from this big trade hadn't yet subsided when on January 3, 1973, a press conference was held in New York to announce the sale of the Yankees by CBS to a group headed by Cleveland shipbuilder George M. Steinbrenner III. Mike Burke would continue as head of the club because, as George put it at the press conference, "I'll stick to building ships and leave the baseball to Lee Mac-Phail and Mike Burke."

A couple of weeks later, the rest of the partners were introduced, including Gabe Paul, who, as general manager of the Cleveland Indians, had just traded Nettles to the Yankees. Mike Burke announced, "Gabe will just stay with us a couple of years, to close out his fine career, and then retire to Florida."

All was not as it appeared.

The CBS era had certainly been a dismal one for the Yankees—the worst in their history since the team was called the Highlanders. Whether the top corporate officers had prevented the Yankees from spending more money on players is purely a matter of speculation. But even if the money had been there, the best players were not necessarily available, and I remember hearing for years how desperately the Yankees wanted Mike Epstein from Washington. As you can see, it might not have been wisely spent even if it had existed.

Steinbrenner, on first introduction, seemed to be the perfect man for the club—a wealthy sportsman whose background included college football coaching, partial ownership of the Chicago Bulls basketball team, a horse farm in Florida, and a love for baseball. He was a highly successful businessman, well known in Cleveland, but lacking national attention. The Yankees would be just the thing to make people notice him, and New York was his kind of town.

When we met in spring training, he seemed eager to get to know who was who, and Gabe Paul seemed like the paternal overseer, not looking to make waves. It was still the Mike-Lee-Ralph show, and we really had no indication of the turbulent era we were entering. All we cared about was getting out of our fourth-place rut, and maybe winning a pennant in the final year of old Yankee Stadium.

Spring training was not without its intrigue. After we'd been in camp only a few days, Fritz Peterson and Mike Kekich, in separate press conferences, announced to the world that they had traded families.

They had called the press conferences because rumor had already begun to leak, and both parties felt that rather than have some wild, untrue rumors hit the papers they'd rather tell the truth. Unfortunately, the truth was wild enough without looking for untrue rumors.

The two couples had been very close friends—we all knew that—but I, at least, never suspected anything strange. After all, however unreal the world of baseball is, it is pretty straight and old-fashioned in terms of marriages and families. The divorce rate is lower than the national average, and most guys seem to marry young, raise families, and avoid "Hollywood" marriages. More often than not, players are married to a girl from back home.

Thinking back now, I really admire the way Mel Stottlemyre handled the news. He was a close friend to both the Petersons and the Kekiches, and knew months before anyone else what had taken place. But, solid citizen that Mel was, he never said a word to anybody, and I know it had to trouble him very much.

I liked both Mike and Fritz, and their wives, too. We had team outings sometimes, like charter boat trips or picnics, and they were always great to have along. But the trading of families made things very strange on the club. To me, if someone fell in love with someone else's wife, well, it's not the ideal situation, but it's something I could understand

and deal with. But the trading of the children—that's something that, from my reference point, I'll never understand. I guess I'm just too close to my children to see how you could ever give them up.

Everyone handled the situation as delicately as possible. The press, of course, blew things out of proportion, which is normal. But the Yankee management, the players, and the principals handled themselves well. There would be no instant trade to send one of them to another team, and as for the players, everyone said, "We're here to play ball, and what they do is their business."

Unfortunately, great strains remained between Mike and Fritz, because misunderstandings developed, and things did not work out well for Kekich and Mrs. Peterson. And although happy-go-lucky Fritz tried to act as if nothing was amiss, the strain between the two couldn't help being felt around the clubhouse.

As we opened the 1973 season, George Steinbrenner was of course there, sitting next to the Yankee dugout. While we lined up along the first baseline for the National Anthem, George began taking notes. He was developing his famous Yankee haircut policy, about ten years behind the times, and certainly out of date in sophisticated New York City.

George was writing down the numbers of the players whose hair, he felt, was too long. Not even the names, mind you, but the numbers, as though that's all we were to him. He sent a note in to Ralph Houk saying the following guys should get haircuts—1, 9, 10, 11, 12, 14, 15, 17, 19, and so on. To Ralph, it was the first sign that some heavy second-guessing would be coming. To us, it made the new owner seem very out of touch with things. But Ralph read us the memo, and some of us got our hair trimmed. A little.

Neither the Yankees nor Thurman Munson got off to a very good start in 1973. The Yankees lost their first four, including three in a row in Fenway Park. I was hitting only

.219 after ten games. And Mike Burke "resigned" when he realized he and George were not destined to get along.

Burke apparently felt he had been betrayed when Gabe Paul emerged. What really transpired is known only by George, Gabe, and Mike, and probably they all remember it differently. But the end result was the departure of Burke and the realization that Gabe Paul was far more important than at first believed. And that George Steinbrenner would not necessarily be sticking to shipbuilding.

But none of us stayed down long. Burke got a terrific settlement from the Yankees and became the head of Madison Square Garden. The Yankees started to win, Munson started to hit, and all the world was happy again.

I brought Diana and the two girls east from Canton in early May to live with me in Westchester County, but no sooner did they arrive than I went into a terrible slump. So I sent them right home, just like that. As I was driving them to the airport, Diana said, "If you get two or three hits tonight, I may never come back." I had three hits and four runs batted in that night and told Nettles, "Who knows, I may be getting divorced!" Just ballplayer humor, but it was a bad year for that kind of joke.

Yankee Stadium was scheduled for a complete remodeling after the season, and for me, it was good news. There were days I wanted to blow the place up. I can't believe it when I see some of the statistics Joe DiMaggio compiled, especially hitting forty-six home runs in one season. The Stadium was a terrible place for a right-handed hitter to make a living, and I'm sure it had done a lot of men in long before I ever arrived on the scene. Really, if you can hit a ball 450 feet and all you get is a long out, something has to be done. I, for one, couldn't wait to get out of Yankee Stadium.

I was hitting the ball harder than I'd done since my rookie year, and despite the long left-field dimensions, I was managing to hit more homers. I was striding differently and really felt my old stroke coming back.

We made big news at the trading deadline of June 15. We had already entered the pennant race, and that morning found ourselves in a virtual tie for first place. Then the Yankees obtained Sam McDowell from the Giants and Pat Dobson from the Braves, two starting pitchers who would step into the rotation at once.

Murcer expressed all of our sentiments when he said, "If we don't win this now, we've got only ourselves to blame." The CBS Yankees had never made such big deals. Now the new ownership was looking pretty good.

McDowell, however, had never been one of my favorites. As a hard-throwing pitcher, he always seemed more interested in embarrassing a hitter than in just retiring him. I didn't respect that, and I didn't change now that I was a teammate. I'd just do my job and call my game. I'm never looking for a strikeout unless it's really needed. When I call a game, it's with a thought to "how can we get this guy to hit off stride, away from his strength."

Dobson, a much craftier pitcher than McDowell, was a guy I really came to admire. First, he was really bright, always working at crossword puzzles, always out to learn. He had already been pitching professionally for fourteen years when we got him, and he still had plenty left. "The Dobber," or "Snake," was a good addition to the club.

And talk about an opinionated guy! Snake had something to say about everything. All of his ideas were well thought out, but it's no surprise that he eventually wore out his welcome with management wherever he pitched. If he felt he had to work on three days' rest and his assignments were coming with four, he'd confront the issue from all corners—manager, general manager, teammates, press, and fans. When Bill Virdon became Yankee manager, Pat wasted no time in arranging for a meeting to tell Virdon his pitching plans. Guys like Dobson will never get high blood pressure or ulcers as long as they keep letting it all out. Or so I'm told, anyway.

When new men come, old ones go, and the arrivals of

these two meant the departure of Kekich. To the Yankees' credit, his departure had nothing to do with the family trade, but it would take a lot of pressure off Peterson and help him, too.

Sure enough, just a couple of days after the 15th, we ran off an eight-game winning streak and moved into first place, building a lead of four games. It was the first time since 1964 that the Yankees had been on top for even a day, and we remained in first place from June 20 until August 1.

This year, it wasn't as hard to see why we were doing so well. Murcer was having another .300 season. Ronnie Blomberg was having a super year, but again hitting against only right-handers. Nettles was giving us power. Jim Ray Hart was filling the DH role for us nicely in the first season of the new rule. Matty Alou, another newcomer, was hitting .300. And we were getting good pitching from Mel, George Medich, Dobson, and particularly Fred Beene in the bullpen.

I like the designated hitter rule, and under the right circumstances, I might let it extend my career a few years. When it comes to rules, I think as a fan does. The fans like a faster game with more action. The DH gives it to them and is much more interesting than watching a pitcher strike out. That's why I like artificial turf, too—a faster game, more action, more excitement.

Sometimes, fans tend to think that players are opposed to change. But the greater consideration is always given to how a particular rule might affect an individual's career. For instance, the designated hitter can extend the career of a batter beyond the time when he's able to play the field well. A pitcher's innings pitched for a season might increase, with fewer pinch-hitting situations called for. But in the long run, it could rob a pitcher of a year or so. Look at Catfish Hunter. I'm not sure his 1975 performance led to his later arm problems, but he pitched thirty complete games in his first Yankee season, and many felt he just threw his arm out that year.

A greater fear is that, one day, rosters might be dropped to twenty-four per team, with the DH rule eliminating the need for an extra hitter or pitcher on the club. That would cost a lot of major league jobs.

Artificial turf doesn't particularly affect the length of a career, but I'd prefer to see some uniformity to the parks, at least in that area. It's really quite a disadvantage to play a team that plays half its games on turf, as opposed to six or so a year. At least the National League has a better balance between natural grass fields and artificial turf.

I made the All-Star team in July, but had to be chosen by Billy Martin, the manager, after Fisk beat me by half a million votes. That bothered me, because I felt he was getting recognition for things I'd already accomplished. A week after the All-Star Game, Fisk and I had a fight during a game in Boston, but it was not triggered by jealousy on either side, just a routine baseball fight over a hard slide. Of course, it gave everyone plenty of additional ammunition to continue talking about our "feud."

By August, we were starting to slip, and the possibility of blowing the season became apparent. When writers started to call the team "gutless," I answered back in defense of the team. Some observers cite that incident as the point when I became a leader of the team. I'd never allow any team I was on to roll over and play dead, as the writers were speculating.

No one was hitting, and the pitching was wearing thin. Lyle, who had done so much for us up to this point, was not working his miracles. I wasn't depressed over my own performance, because I was still giving 100 percent every day, but I was unhappy with the way we were playing as a team.

We started the month of August tied for first. By the end of the month, we had lost eighteen of twenty-seven, and had dropped nine and a half games from the top into fourth place. There would be no catching up.

The final month of the old Yankee Stadium was one of the worst I've lived through. The fans were on us every day, especially on Ralph. We played just as badly in September as we had in August, and fell hopelessly out of the race. In the end, we didn't even finish at .500, and our fourth-place finish (again) left us seventeen games from the top.

Those of us who were closest to Houk knew that the fans were in fact getting to him. Ralph never liked to lose, but for years now he'd fallen short of a pennant, despite getting all he could out of his teams. He also felt new restraints placed on him by the new ownership, and the confidence which had been shown in him no longer seemed a certainty.

Ralph resigned following the final game of the season, which we lost 8–5 to Detroit. The fans were never worse than they were during that game, which was the last to be played in the old Stadium. It pained me when Ralph was forced to come out and make a pitching change late in the game. He got a terrible booing and walked back to the dugout like a beaten man.

He had tears in his eyes when he spoke to us in the clubhouse about his decision, and they were genuine, because he had spent his entire adult life with the Yankees. But, as he said, perhaps a change would be better for everyone. The season had been one of the most disappointing, and although it was said that a great effort was made to get him to change his mind, the management accepted his decision. Personally, I couldn't see how any manager could be better. Maybe he was a little too easy sometimes, but he treated everyone like a man and got the most out of people. I was really upset by his decision.

Of course, baseball goes on, and only the characters change. A few weeks later, Ralph was his old smiling self again, signing to manage the Detroit Tigers. And Lee MacPhail was the newly elected president of the American League. An era had ended.

A HITTER NAMED
DAVE SCHNECK

Statistically, the 1973 season had been one of my best. I batted .301 and hit twenty home runs despite all my complaining about Yankee Stadium, so most people figured I'd improve on that when we got out of there.

It was a pleasant off-season for me. I had really learned to relax in 1973, both when we were doing well and when we weren't. I think this made me a more capable catcher. By now, I had four years under my belt and was regarded as a veteran—a man who knew the hitters well enough to be turned to for guidance by a pitching staff.

I was playing golf in a tournament in Puerto Rico that November when news reached us that the Yankees were naming Dick Williams as Ralph's replacement. As it turned out, this was just the first of an endless line of moves that the new ownership would make, few of which went smoothly.

Williams had built a reputation as a brilliant manager by first leading Boston to a miracle pennant in 1967, and then guiding the Oakland A's to a pair of World Championships. He quit after the 1973 Series, seemingly tired of getting dictated to by Charlie Finley and being told whom to play. He felt the Yankees were more ideally suited to letting him run things his own way. As Billy Martin found out in later years, Dick would have been very wrong.

Everything was in a state of chaos at the time, so it was not surprising that things didn't work out well. Gabe Paul was now a formidable power on the Yankees and had become the general manager, to no one's surprise. Lee MacPhail was in his final weeks with the club, for he would soon be elected American League President to replace the retiring Joe Cronin. And George Steinbrenner was becoming deeply involved in the growing Watergate scandal, he being named through his shipping business as an illegal campaign contributor to the 1972 Nixon re-election fund.

Then Charlie Finley announced he wouldn't let Dick Williams manage the Yankees, because he still had a contract with Oakland. Many people felt he was just irritating a long-time foe, Gabe Paul, who had once raided his front office to bring Phil Seghi to Cleveland.

In the midst of this confusion, Houk signed to manage the Tigers. And, of course, Ralph had resigned with a couple of years remaining on his Yankee contract, just as Williams had left Oakland.

Finley decided that if he was going to let Williams go, he'd get some compensation. He insisted that for the Yankees to keep Williams they'd have to give him Scott McGregor, a left-handed pitcher, and Otto Velez, an outfielder, both from the Syracuse team.

"McGregor and Velez?" said Gabe Paul. "They're our crown jewels! We're not giving them up."

McGregor never made it to the Yankees, finally getting his chance with Baltimore in 1977. Velez moved up and down between the Yankees and Syracuse before Toronto drafted him in 1976.

So the Yankees wouldn't give any players for Williams, and you can't blame Finley for trying. A few years later, he managed to get Manny Sanguillen from the Pirates for his manager, Chuck Tanner.

Without his compensation, Finley said, Williams could manage anyone but the Yankees, as far as he was concerned. The matter went before Joe Cronin, and in his final decision as American League President, he ruled that Houk could go to the Tigers but Williams could not go to the Yankees. I've never understood the difference, and when MacPhail succeeded Cronin a few weeks later, he admitted that he would have ruled differently.

As we headed for the winter meetings, we had no manager and unstable leadership. MacPhail was gone, and Tal Smith was brought in from Houston, seemingly as a replacement. A big press conference was held to give the impression that Tal was the new general manager, but in fact Gabe was now running the show.

Steinbrenner, to add to the confusion, was on the verge of being suspended by Commissioner Kuhn after he was found guilty of illegal campaign contributions. His fine was a light one, and he had come out of the episode rather heroically, explaining how the Committee to Re-Elect the President had applied undue pressure on him to secure the contributions. But Kuhn felt that Steinbrenner, now a convicted felon, was an undesirable, and he was forbidden to have anything to do with the running of the club.

I was keeping up with all of this merriment through the newspapers. Like the fans, I was certainly anxious to find out who the new manager would be, and had to admit to being disappointed at losing Williams, who had said some highly complimentary things about me at his press conference.

Back in New York, plans were being made to shift operations to Shea Stadium, which we would share with the Mets for two years.

At last came the announcement of the new manager. It would be Bill Virdon, who had managed the Pirates for the previous two seasons before getting fired while in the midst of a pennant race.

Bill was certainly a surprise choice for the job. He had been in the National League for the past twenty years as a player, coach, and manager. His tie to the Yankees was minimal—he had begun his career as a minor league player in the Yankee organization, but had been traded to the Cardinals in 1954. He was certainly nothing like Dick Williams, who was a flashy, newsy manager, always visible.

Virdon was very reserved, with traditional, mid-American values. Running a baseball team meant setting rules and seeing that everyone followed the rules. I knew he had gotten into some trouble with his Pirate players—Richie Hebner and Dock Ellis—by sticking too rigidly to his rule system. He was not a personality boy, and could go weeks without speaking to you, for no other reason than he had nothing to say. But I knew him only by reputation, and was prepared to approach the situation with an open mind. I didn't want to appear unable to adjust to a change, certainly not after four years in the majors at the age of twenty-six.

Bill Virdon kept a very low profile. At one point during the season, he went almost three weeks without saying anything to anyone. This, of course, didn't include his mound conferences, but even those were minimal. He preferred to send Whitey Ford to the mound.

He even preferred to send Dick Howser to the plate with the lineup. At one point, he was almost invisible to the fans, but I think the front office finally told him to at least make an appearance on the field.

When Bill would get into an argument, he was just as hot as any other manager, and it was a completely different man we'd see running onto the field—almost a complete stranger. It was so out of character to see him talk, let alone argue. He was normally so reserved.

Anyway, we were going through this period of little com-

munication, and then one day, as we passed his office individually on our way to the field, he called us each in.

"Thurman," I heard as I headed past. In I went. "Here,
sign these would you?"

Some kid had mailed in a bunch of pictures of the Yankees for autographs, addressed to Bill, and he had spread
them over his desk for us to sign as we went by.

Bill had one guy he'd talk to all the time, and that was
his coach, Mel Wright. Mel didn't seem to be around for any
reason other than to keep Bill company. Even today, with
Bill managing in Houston, there's Mel right by his side. He
did develop a good rapport with Tal Smith, though, and
that's how he eventually landed the Houston job. Tal went
there as general manager in 1975.

I don't mean to put Virdon down. He knew baseball, and
he did his job as best he saw it. It was just that I didn't develop the same closeness with him that I had with Houk,
and I missed it.

Bill would always insist on my taking batting practice
and infield practice, for instance. Now, I'm one of the biggest advocates of batting practice there is. I don't kid
around in the cage—I really get ready for a game. I use a
heavier bat than I do in a game, and it forces me to really
roll my wrists as I swing. This is the secret of hitting, and
batting practice is not a place to fool around.

But there are times when I'll make a personal decision
that because I am tired, because I may have caught ten or
twelve games in a row, I'd rather relax before the game.
This was never in line with Bill's thinking. It always had to
be his way.

I remember on plane trips the way we'd almost have to
hide like children if we were drinking a beer. We were almost embarrassed to look at Bill if we were holding a beer,
because he wasn't a beer drinker, and there was something
about him that made us feel guilty.

I signed my 1974 contract on February 3 for $75,000,

which made me the highest-paid catcher in Yankee history. Of course, the salary standards were already changing, and in no way was I ready to stand beside Bill Dickey, Yogi Berra, or Elston Howard yet. Gene Michael was the highest-paid shortstop in Yankee history, and he'd be the first to tell you that he couldn't compare to Phil Rizzuto. Phil would be the second to tell you.

I was pleased with the good raise, happy to be moving into Shea Stadium, and eager for the season to begin. Unfortunately, spring training held for me a fateful day in my career which would affect my play for years to come.

It was April 2 in Columbia, South Carolina. We were there on our way north, playing the New York Mets in the third-to-last exhibition game of the season. We were playing there because Bobby Richardson was the coach of the University of South Carolina, and he had set up the game. As you can imagine, quite a crowd was on hand.

The Mets had an outfielder named Dave Schneck with them that season. He was a twenty-four year old left-hand hitter, who had been with the Mets briefly the previous two seasons, and who would play regularly for them in 1974. His lifetime batting average in the majors would be .199.

Schneck's first time at bat, he swung hard, followed through, and hit me in my bare hand with his backswing. The bat crashed into me right where the thumb and the forefinger come together. I dropped to my knees in pain, but stayed in the game and played four more innings. Catchers are always getting banged up, and usually the pain doesn't come on until after a game, when the swelling maximizes and the bruise comes out. I've had a lot of foul balls bounce off me, and the normal catching injuries. At first, this one seemed like just another one.

At bat, Jon Matlack jammed me with a pitch, and the very act of holding the bat suddenly pained me. I came out of the game, and Gene Monahan checked me out. We had some X-rays taken, but they didn't reveal anything.

We finished spring training, and I was in the starting lineup on opening day in New York. Stottlemyre beat Gaylord Perry 6–1, but I definitely didn't feel right. By the second game, my hand was killing me. It was getting worse, not better.

A few weeks later, we were playing the White Sox, and Carlos May crashed into my thumb sliding home. That aggravated the injury, and I was out for ten days. I came back, was involved in another play at the plate, and missed another week.

What was going on in my arm was a severe inflammation of the medial nerve. The pain in my thumb was so severe that it was impossible for me to grip the ball properly in throwing. My thumb played almost no part in holding objects. It hurt just to lift a cup of coffee, and shaking hands was about the most painful thing of all.

Naturally, my throwing was greatly affected. Sometimes, it would amaze me that I'd be able to reach second base at all. It didn't take long for word to get around that Munson wasn't throwing right, and the once accurate arm, which generally fired shots to second in a three-quarter delivery, was now getting throws to second sidearm—almost underarm. The action contributed to the development of bursitis in my right shoulder, and physically I was really a mess.

It would drive Rick Dempsey, our backup catcher, absolutely crazy to see me throwing so poorly, with him sitting in the bullpen. But calling a game remained far more important than throwing runners out, and our pitching staff stood behind me solidly. I made twenty-two errors that season, but in the end, the players voted me a second consecutive Gold Glove Award. A lot of people thought that was foolish, but the fine points of a game like calling pitches are never appreciated by the casual observer.

The arm injury was long-lasting. Looking back today, I wish I had rested more in 1974. I caught 144 games, all with pain, and probably pushed myself too hard. More rest might have helped the healing process. By the following spring, I still had an unnatural tingling in my fingers, and I thought I was going to need an operation. I even had neurological tests conducted.

Not until 1977 did my arm finally return to its top form, and was I able to return to throwing three-quarters.

The '74 season was really a wheeling-dealing year, the first with Gabe in full charge. We used forty-four different players that season, including nineteen pitchers. The biggest surprise occurred on April 26, remembered by those who were there as the Friday Night Massacre.

We had just beaten Texas in Shea Stadium for Stottlemyre's fourth win of the young season. Mel was off to his best start, and the team was just half a game out of first. The night game had ended, and up in the press box, a major trade was being announced.

The Yankees had traded four of their eight pitchers—Fritz Peterson, Fred Beene, Steve Kline, and Tom Buskey—to the Indians for Chris Chambliss, Dick Tidrow, and Cecil Upshaw.

It was really a shock. Half the pitching staff was gone, just like that. Beene was the guy I felt worst about—he was some kind of middle-inning relief man. Upshaw, who would replace him, could never approach the job he was doing.

The team reacted with a measure of anger. First of all, the timing was awful. We were doing well, had just won a game, and now here comes the press into the clubhouse, wanting everyone's comments about the trade, while Fritz, Steve, Freddy, and Tom faced the trauma of a move. In that awful little room which had been assigned to us, chaos seemed the order of the day. And here came Gabe Paul, a big smile on his face, right into the clubhouse, as though the friendships of the four men he'd traded didn't mean anything to us.

The Cleveland connection bothered us. It seemed as

though Paul and Steinbrenner, both being from Cleveland, were bringing the whole Indian team here. First were Nettles, Jerry Moses, and Walt Williams, then this shipload. Plus, we had Sam McDowell, Lou Piniella, Fred Stanley— all veterans of the Indians' organization.

I suppose we all said more than we might have if we'd had time to think things through, myself included. We were far more openly critical of the deal than we would have been had we been asked for opinions a day later.

Chambliss felt a little unwelcome in New York although none of us acted less than friendly toward him. But it took him a full season to adjust, and his lack of hitting hurt us in 1974.

Maybe had we known Chris a little better we could have helped to ease his transition. It's always hard for a player to be traded in midseason. One day you're with one team, the next day another. No time to really think about it, and no time to consider the change in loyalties.

Of course, you also have the problem of moving and family considerations. Chris' wife, Audrey, was happy in Cleveland, had been writing a newspaper column there, and Chris felt he was becoming a fixture on the Indians. Suddenly, it's all over. Chris is a sensitive guy, and doesn't have the devil-may-care attitude of a Sparky Lyle that would enable him to shrug his shoulders and say, "Okay it's a new day." His need to adjust to the new situation was probably a very normal reaction, which those of us in baseball tend to ignore. I don't think Audrey was very happy at first in New York, either, which couldn't have helped matters. Baseball players can be close in terms of companionship, but for deeper needs, like having a friend to sit down with and discuss real unhappiness, the nature of the sport and its movement of athletes inhibits this. I suspect Chris could have used someone to talk to during that '74 season.

Later, of course, both he and Tidrow became important

members of our championship clubs, so in retrospect, it was a good trade. At the time, trading half the pitching staff right after spring training just seemed crazy.

Late in spring training, the Yankees obtained Elliott Maddox from Texas. This was at first a minor deal for a reserve outfielder. But Virdon, a former center fielder himself, immediately took a liking to Maddox' defensive abilities, which he had plenty of. Within a few weeks, he installed Elliott in center and moved Bobby Murcer to right. Bobby wasn't too happy with the move, and never had a great admiration for Virdon after that. Elliott, of course, thought Virdon was great, and went on to justify Bill's confidence by hitting over .300. A year later, though, Maddox got hurt, and has yet to return to that 1974 form. A shame, but part of baseball.

I'll tell you what's a real shame, and in many ways, it's what baseball is all about. It's why players look to make a lot of money when they can, because it can all end so suddenly, and no matter what you've done, you're nothing when it's over.

Mel Stottlemyre, one of the really class guys in the organization, had won twenty games three times with mediocre clubs. He was the last remaining player from the pennant era, and had maintained the Yankee class during all the hard years. He was as steady as they went, and a pitcher can be a tremendous asset to a club just by going out there every four or five days and giving you eight or nine innings, win or lose. It stabilizes the whole staff. That was Mel, a stabilizing force. He was our pitching leader, and a man to respect. And when he was throwing right, he was as good as Catfish Hunter, Whitey Ford—you name 'em.

Mel's greatest success over the years had come at the expense of the California Angels, and so we were all expecting an easy game when we met them a June evening in Shea Stadium.

But after just a couple of innings, Mel threw a pitch and

reached for his shoulder. I went to the mound, with Virdon and trainer Gene Monahan close behind from the dugout.

Monahan did most of the speaking, as I recall, telling Mel to do this and do that and to see if it hurt. It did, but Mel decided to stay in and finish the inning.

For Mel Stottlemyre, it was all over. It was as though each man is blessed with just a certain number of pitches in his arm, and Mel's quota had expired. He had a torn rotator cuff in his right shoulder. He went on the disabled list, came back in August to make one brief relief appearance, and never pitched again. Just like that, a career was finished.

The following spring, Mel was still on the roster, and when he reported to camp, he was told to take as much time as he needed to get ready. In fact, he was told not to push himself toward opening day—if necessary, he could stay behind in Florida and get ready at his own pace.

Mel took that at its word and threw slowly, bringing his arm around at his own speed. Then, as spring training was winding down, the Yankees released him. An outright release—a pink slip. Did you know that when a player is released he actually has to sign his own release form?

It was late afternoon, well after the workout and well after the writers had departed, when Mel was asked to return to the Fort Lauderdale Stadium offices.

In all the years I knew Stottlemyre, I never knew him to speak a bad word about anybody. But this time, he was furious. He felt he had been lied to. Had he been told he had to be ready by such and such a date, he'd have gone about things differently.

As it was, Mel really couldn't pitch anymore. Houk would have signed him in a minute for Detroit had he been able to throw, but he couldn't. So the incident left a bad taste with everyone, and despite all those grand years he'd given the Yankees, his services were no longer desired in any capacity. Here's a man who should have had a position in the or-

ganization, but the bitter departure caused another ex-
Yankee to harbor bad feelings. I doubt we'll see Mel at an
Old Timer's game in the near future.

Despite my arm troubles, the Yankees played good baseball in 1974. No one expected as much from the club as it
turned out we had. But the race was close again. In May, we
were in first place with only an 18-15 record. Then we went
into a slump and fell to last place, holding down the cellar
from June 26 to July 10. For a while, every game seemed
like a road game. Shea Stadium should have been a better
park to hit in, we felt. Murcer couldn't hit one out of
there—and didn't, in fact, until September. What seemed to
keep us going was the great pitching of Doc Medich and Pat
Dobson, Sparky's relief work, the hitting of Maddox and
Lou Piniella, and good infield play by Jim Mason and
Sandy Alomar.

The arrival of Piniella onto the scene brought me a really
close friend. Lou's a real beauty. He's one of the best hitters
I've ever seen, and a guy who can talk hitting twenty-four
hours a day if you'll let him. Yet while his average bears
him out as one of the top hitters in baseball, he's the most
self-critical player I've ever seen. He doesn't seem to have
any appreciation of his own abilities.

Lou is very popular with fans because they all think he's
the same nationality as they are. Especially the Italians—
they're convinced he's Italian. But in fact Lou is Spanish—as in from Spain. Castilian. And he speaks fluent
Spanish, too. Sometimes, he'll get into an argument with
an umpire and begin to swear in Spanish.

He was the first hero they ever had in Kansas City,
where the fans would greet his arrival at bat with cheers of
"Lou! Lou!" It took on the aura of a bullfight ring, which
was appropriate. The New York fans picked up on that, too,
but sometimes it would be hard to tell the "Lou" sound from
a "boo." Piniella always assumed it was the former.

Not long after he got to camp, he was introduced to Celerino Sanchez and pressed into duty as a translator for his contract talks with Gabe Paul. It was a funny scene, Piniella and Sanchez having just met, and now Lou was virtually serving as Cellie's agent.

Piniella's voice, in English or Spanish, is a little shrill, especially when he gets mad. It's got a nasal sound, too, and it just doesn't sound like it's coming out of his 200-pound body. People love to mimic him when he gets mad, and that always gets him laughing.

Mason was very young—young enough to make me feel old, anyway, but he gave us a good season in 1974, hitting 250 and fielding very well, especially when Alomar arrived to play second. But after that first season, Jim got really messed up. He forgot how to hit, he forgot how to field, and the more worried he became, the worse he became. Finally, the fans were on him so badly he virtually quit. What a blessing it was for the Mase when he finally got out of New York.

Fans can really get to you—I know, because they've gotten to me. In New York, despite the big Stadium and the big crowds, you can hear what's said. You wouldn't believe some of the language people pour on you—especially as you're entering or leaving the Stadium. When you're on deck, people will run right up to the rail and call you the most vile names you've ever heard. And, of course, we always pretend we don't hear them.

One time in particular, in 1976, it really got to me. I'd been hitting really well, but on this one play against Oakland, I threw a ball into centerfield and Don Baylor scored. The scoring wasn't my fault—he went to third thanks to me, but when I struck out an inning later, some fans by the dugout really let me have it. I was really frustrated, and in a moment of anger, I delivered a well-recognized obscene gesture at them.

It may not have been the classiest move I ever made, but you'd be surprised what happened. The majority of fans understood my frustration, and the next day, I got a tremendous hand when I came up. I'd say normally a crowd would never forgive a player for what I did. But in my case, they got behind me like never before. It was quite a thing, and really justified my belief that, basically, New York fans are great. They're the most knowledgeable, the most appreciative, and they've always been super to me.

I lost the All-Star election in 1974 to Fisk by half a million votes, again, but he was disabled, and I started the game for the first time. It was played in Pittsburgh, and I caught the whole game, handling Gaylord Perry, Luis Tiant, Rollie Fingers, and that man from the A's, Catfish Hunter. Hunter was the easiest of the four to handle, but the Nationals scored off each of them, and we lost again, 7–2.

Back in the regular season, a couple of late-arriving pitchers—Rudy May and Larry Gura—began to pitch well for us, and by the middle of August, we were starting to win. Fortunately, we had never fallen more than eight and a half games out of first, and so when we won eighteen of twenty-eight in August and nineteen of twenty-nine in September, we were suddenly in another pennant race.

Although my hand was hurting and tendonitis had inevitably settled in, I started to hit much better in September. On the 4th, George Medich won his seventeenth game and moved us into a tie with Boston for the lead. We split a four-game series with Detroit to remain tied, including a terrific 1–0 win in which Gura beat Fryman.

Then we went to Fenway Park for two typical Yankee-Red Sox pennant pressure games. That's when baseball is great. Boston is a great baseball town, and the Yankee-Red Sox rivalry really keeps it that way. They've got some of the best fans in the world there, and I liked it even when I was playing in the Cape Cod League. In fact, I remember that all the fans at our Cape Cod League games

would bring radios with them so they could listen to the
Boston games.

Also, I really like to hit in Fenway Park, which is a great
park for a right-hand hitter if you don't let the wall psyche
you out. I've seen that happen with people who get overanx-
ious to play that wall.

Not surprisingly, we drew more than 68,000 people for
the two games, in a park which only seats a little more than
30,000. It seems every time we play there, we set a new attendance record.

We won the first game 6–3, beating an old nemesis, Roger
Moret, and in a real thriller, took the second game 2–1 in
twelve innings—Alex Johnson, playing his first game for
the Yankees, homered in the twelfth. It was one of those
games that really make you feel you're the team of destiny.

Everybody was singing Bill Virdon's praises now, but we
were so hot it was as though we were out of anyone's control.

We played a doubleheader in Baltimore on September 11,
losing 3–2 in seventeen innings, and then winning 5–1 behind Gura to hold onto a two-game lead. I was stinging the
ball now, and finally feeling as though I was making a contribution. I knew as well as anyone that if I'd only been able
to play healthy all year, we might have a bigger lead, but
there wasn't much I could do about it.

Off we went to Detroit, where it must have given Houk a
lot of mixed feelings to see us on top the year after he'd left.
And he told everyone that he would rather see us win than
Boston or Baltimore, because he knew so many of us. I wonder how he really felt.

We took two of three in Detroit to build the lead to two
and a half games, and headed home to play Baltimore,
Cleveland, and Boston. I don't know whether it was just a
bad year for New York baseball or whether our fans just
couldn't adapt to Shea Stadium, but our crowds were really

disappointing for those ten big games. Today, 40,000 or more would be at Yankee Stadium, but only one of those games topped the 40,000 mark, and in four of them we failed to draw 25,000. We really had to wonder what was keeping everyone home.

As it was, we were done in right at the start of the home-stand. The Orioles stopped us cold, beating us 4–0, 10–4 and 7–0 behind Palmer, Cuellar, and McNally, an old story. Yet the sweep left us only one-half game out of first with twelve to play, and it was still a race.

Around this time, George Steinbrenner, the suspended owner, sent a tape-recorded message into the clubhouse for Virdon to play. It felt very high schoolish, but we couldn't blame George for his enthusiasm, and it was good to know he was a fan.

The Indians were in a position to knock us off if they could get up for the games, because we had four with them at home and three in Cleveland. At times like that, a team either will get inspired to figure in the pennant race, or, if it's not battling for anything in particular, may play dead. Cleveland came closer to the latter.

We took four in a row in Shea Stadium from the Indians, to move back into first, but with only a one-game lead. This was really pennant pressure, and we were loving it. It sure beat going through the motions in the dog days of September.

Now the Red Sox came to town for a doubleheader, and they broke our backs with 4–0 and 4–2 victories behind Tiant and Moret. We dropped to second, half a game behind the Orioles.

Medich won his nineteenth the next day, beating Bill Lee 1–0, but the Orioles won also, and we were still half a game out with five left to play.

Off we went to Cleveland, to play in damp and dismal weather before depressingly small crowds of just over 8,000. We were rained out on Friday night as the Orioles beat Detroit to build the lead to one, but on Saturday, we took a doubleheader 9–3 and 9–7, with Steinbrenner dancing in the aisles behind the Yankee dugout. He always wanted us to look our best in Cleveland, where his business and family were.

Still, it seemed as though every time we won, the Orioles won, and although that had been going on for only a few days, it felt like months.

Now it was Sunday, and Rudy May pitched against Fritz Peterson, our old teammate. We knew Fritz would be up to beat us, but it was not to be. We knocked him out early and coasted to a 10–0 victory. As we flew back to New York after the game, all the talk was about how Houk, in Baltimore, could have walked a man to face Tommy Davis in the Oriole-Tiger game. Davis, the old pro, came through with the game-winning hit, and we were still one game out with two to play.

The two remaining games were to be in Milwaukee. Even if we won them both, the Orioles could clinch by winning two.

We had been counted out when the Orioles swept us three straight, and again when we lost the doubleheader to the Red Sox. But here we were, still clinging to life with two games left. If we won it, it would be super. If we didn't, we'd have given them one helluva race, and had nothing to be ashamed of.

We stayed in New York for a day and a half and then flew to Milwaukee. It was not a smooth trip. When we got to the hotel in Milwaukee, Rick Dempsey and Bill Sudakis, my two backup catchers, got into a fight right in the lobby. It was a ridiculous situation, and to make matters worse, Bobby Murcer tried to break it up and got himself hurt. Bobby was not in the lineup that night, and we could have used him.

The Brewers beat us 3–2 in ten innings on a single by George Scott. Medich didn't have his best stuff in going for

his twentieth win, but he pitched valiantly, knowing what
was at stake. I remember how odd it was to be playing such
a big game and to have 4,000 people in the stands.

We won 2–1 the next day to finish the season with
eighty-nine victories, two behind Baltimore. We had given
them a fight.

I wound up the year with twenty hits in my last forty-
nine at-bats, a .408 average, and although my arm didn't
feel much better, I thought I had at least salvaged some of
the season by being an important participant in the pennant drive. But for the season, I'd hit a dismal .261, with
only thirteen home runs and sixty runs batted in—after everyone was so sure my home run potential would increase
in Shea Stadium.

With the season over, all I wanted to do was go home and
rest. I had no desire to lift a bat, or even a golf club. I had
played in pain, and didn't like it.

HUNTER, BONDS AND BATTLIN' BILLY

If I hadn't known what a disappointing season I'd had just by feeling the pain, it became clear enough when the Yankees sent me my contract for 1975. Today, a player is paid just for playing—for what he can give you in terms of durability and what he's worth *not* to be with someone else. But back then, players were still paid totally on performance, and I didn't have much to argue about. I got a small raise.

I kept in touch with our trainer Gene Monahan all winter, and avoided doing anything that might have been bothersome to my right hand and arm. I even gave up golf, which is one of my favorite pastimes. I'm not a bad player, and enjoy competing in the baseball player tournaments held each winter.

I was pretty concerned about my future. There was no way that I wanted to continue a lengthy career if it required playing in pain. I can appreciate why Sandy Koufax quit while he was on top. No money can make the risk of permanent injury worthwhile.

Just a few weeks after the World Series ended—October 22, to be exact—Gabe Paul woke up Bobby Murcer at his home in Oklahoma City with some startling news. Bobby had been traded to the San Francisco Giants for Bobby Bonds. It was called the biggest one-for-one trade in baseball history.

To Murcer, it was a heck of a shock. Only a few weeks earlier, he'd been told by the front office that there was no thought of trading him and he could count on being a Yankee for a long time. As the team's "crown prince," having inherited the legacy of Ruth, Gehrig, DiMaggio, and Mantle by virtue of his publicity buildup, he seemed destined to be a Yankee always. He was popular with the fans, never caused trouble, and had become a terrific player, both offensively and defensively.

Bobby was the glamour boy of the team, and a great personal friend of mine. Those who listened to Reggie Jackson talking about my supposed jealousy of him a few years later should think back to the days when Bobby and I, along with Roy White, were the only players on the club hitting regularly. I could certainly have had the same jealousy back then if it was in my nature, because Bobby always had the headlines, and I just went out and did my job. But we had a terrific relationship, and I knew I'd miss him a lot. We still talk on the phone very often during the season.

The lesson I learned with Bobby's trade was that you can never predict anything in baseball. One day they say he'll be a Yankee forever, and the next day he's gone. I can't fault the club for making an attractive deal, but I wish Bobby hadn't been misled.

Make no mistake about it, Bonds was a super athlete. For his combination of speed and power, few could touch him. He was coming off a bad year—for him—and the Yankees jumped at the chance to snare a man they felt was one of the five or six best players in the game.

While everyone was talking about Bobby Bonds, more news came across the radio. Jim "Catfish" Hunter, against whom I'd made my big league debut back in 1969, had been declared a free agent by an arbitration panel.

Catfish had announced this during the World Series, but no one took him seriously. It was a simple matter—his boss, Charlie Finley, had breached his contract by failing to pay him promised money. It could have happened anytime—it was purely coincidental that it came one year before the Messersmith-McNally decision, which shook the reserve clause—but the timing was such that it will probably be remembered as the historic first free agent incident. And, of course, since he was one of the best pitchers in baseball, his free agency established a price scale for future free agents.

As soon as he was officially declared a free agent and so proclaimed by the commissioner, the bidding was on. Only someone as cool as Catfish could sit back on his farm in Hertford, North Carolina, and keep from jumping at the quickly rising prices. Everyone wondered how much it would take. A couple of hundred thousand? Perhaps even a million? No one could be sure, but one thing was certain. More than twenty clubs were interested, and that got the stakes up in a hurry.

Neither Catfish nor his lawyers had any idea what the price would finally be. But it was quite a show that followed. Representatives of most of the clubs headed for Ahoskie, North Carolina, to make a personal pitch to Catfish's lawyers.

I developed a real rooting interest. Hell, we were two games out in 1974—the addition of Hunter could really put us over the top. You can never have enough pitching, and to add a guy like Hunter would really be a bonus. I decided to do what I could, so I telephoned him a few times to talk up the Yankees.

He was his usual cool self on the phone. The ol' country boy, listening to the bids, enjoying the action. I don't know if my calls did any good—Cat later said they helped—but I know the key to his decision to sign with the Yankees was his long time friendship with Clyde Kluttz.

Clyde, as nice a man as I've ever met, was a Kansas City scout when he found Hunter back in 1964. He didn't quit on

Jimmy when a hunting accident cost Hunter the small toe on his right foot and he got him a nice bonus. The two Southern boys became good friends, and a warm trust developed.

Clyde was now running the Yankees' scouting operation, and he was the man on the scene in Ahoskie, pursuing Hunter once again. Gabe Paul flew down a couple of times to do the heavy business, but in the end, it was the friendship between Kluttz and Hunter that brought Jimmy to New York.

The price was high, and it included a bonus, lawyer's fees, and life insurance over and above a high salary—arrangements which were precedent-setting for the future. Of course, no one knew what the future held. This was considered a once-in-a-lifetime event, and Hunter was the beneficiary. The press reported his total package was worth almost $3 million.

So there we were—a team that barely missed the 1974 pennant, now armed with Catfish Hunter's arm and Bobby Bonds' bat. No way we could miss, right?

Spring training proceeded at its normal pace. Bill Virdon, who had been named Manager of the Year by *The Sporting News,* seemed more comfortable, more in control. Those of us who had gone through the pennant race felt more mature in a baseball sense. Very confident, too.

All eyes were on Hunter, of course. Even Bobby Bonds had a much less pressured spring than he would have without Hunter along. Everywhere we played, people wanted to see Catfish. We sold out almost every park we played in.

I know Gabe Paul didn't think we took spring training seriously, but we never felt that way. Virdon worked us harder than Houk ever did, including double workout sessions. That meant the squad would split in half, and everyone would get more individual time. It was especially tough on the coaching staff, because they were involved in both the morning and the afternoon sessions.

Steinbrenner would come around as a fan and have virtually nothing to do with us. He'd sit by the dugout and cheer,
but he was obeying Commissioner Kuhn's banishment to
the letter, hoping his good behavior would result in a light-
er sentence.

We wound up the training season with fourteen wins in
thirty-one games—not very impressive, but, then, spring
records don't mean a thing. You play the games differently—you don't pinch-hit in the late innings, you don't make
defensive changes, you don't play your regulars. A lot of
fans get all excited about spring records, but even a proven
hitter who bats .125 in spring training usually isn't concerned. It's mostly a question of getting into playing shape.

We played two games with the Pirates in San Juan that
spring for the benefit of Roberto Clemente's Sports City, a
developing athletic complex for youngsters, and that was
like a homecoming for me.

When we broke camp and headed north, Virdon named
Doc Medich to pitch the opener in Cleveland, saving Catfish
for the home opener on Friday in New York.

Doc had won nineteen the year before, losing that game
in Milwaukee at the end of the season in a bid for his twentieth. That turned out to be his peak season. He always
spent too much time messing around on the mound. He'd go
three and two on everyone, it seemed. A very slow worker.
From then on, as he got closer to his M.D. from the University of Pittsburgh, his mind seemed more on medicine than
baseball.

This was no ordinary day in Cleveland. It was Frank Robinson's debut as a manager, the first black manager in
baseball. Mrs. Jackie Robinson was there, Bowie Kuhn was
there, and even more impressive, almost 57,000 fans were
there. I hadn't seen Cleveland Municipal Stadium that full
since I was a kid. It had always been so depressing to play
in that giant stadium before three or four thousand fans.
The weather was nasty on this particular day, but every-

one's adrenaline was pumping good, considering the historic occasion and the big crowd.

Robinson made himself the designated hitter, and in the bottom of the first, he grabbed hold of one of Doc's pitches and rammed it into the left field seats like a shot. It was one of the most incredible sights I've ever seen at a ball park. Robby stopped at home and waved his helmet, and fans poured onto the field. News cameras were all over the place. When an opponent hits a home run, as a rule you just shuffle the dirt, get a new ball, and try to hurry on to the next hitter. But this was an event that had to be watched— it was a great day for baseball.

We lost the game 5–3, which didn't cause anyone much concern. We felt we had contributed to a very special day in Cleveland, Ohio.

Catfish pitched the home opener in Shea Stadium against Detroit on Friday. Only 26,000 fans turned out, convincing me we just didn't have drawing power in Shea Stadium. There was no way we could establish an identity there. Mickey Lolich beat us 5–3 and we were 0–2. But it was good for Hunter, with all the amazing news attention, to get his first start out of the way.

As I've said, our locker room in Shea was very small. It was the same one assigned to the New York Jets, and I'll never understand how forty big football players could have used it. It was hard enough for the twenty-five of us, but with the crush of newsmen following Hunter, it was ridiculous. The entire center of the room was filled with cameras, lights, and sportswriters, interviewing one another while they waited for Hunter to finish icing his arm. The ritual continued almost all season, and it really got on my nerves after a while. There were times after a tough loss when I just hated to come in and see that mass of humanity swarming around. Those were the days when I made good use of my reputation as a grouch.

Writers always said I was grumpy and surly. This image grew out of my sarcastic sense of humor, which goes over all right among players, but writers don't usually understand it. So when I'd give gruff and angry answers early in my career, they'd write stories about how grouchy I was.

It would bother Diana to see this in print, but it didn't bother me. If they had legitimate questions to ask, I'd always answer. But more often than not, they would just ask ridiculous questions to get a story no one else had. With so many writers around New York—at least two dozen on any given day—they always have to come up with different angles. And the next day, when they read one another's stories, they check if they've missed something controversial, and continue that line of questioning. It seems to me to be a poor method of journalism. And, of course, having seen some of the stories they'd done on other players, I was determined to avoid that. I began to enjoy seeing writers bother *other* players with dumb questions.

So I became a "grouch." My teammates knew better, and my family knew better, and that's all I was concerned with. And if being a grouch meant people wouldn't bother me with silly questions and silly requests, then it worked to my benefit.

Catfish had a much better temperament than I. He'd give everyone the same answers, all polite and all to the point. The only person he'd ever rip would be Finley, and he even did that in good humor. I admired his ability to handle it all, especially considering his background—coming from a small town in North Carolina and playing for so many years in Kansas City and Oakland.

And things were rough for Cat that month. He lost his second start on April 15, Boston beating him 5–3 in front of 7,773 fans in Shea. And then Lolich beat him again, 8–3 in Detroit. The Cat was now 0–3, and we were 2–7. People were wondering what was happening. And we were saying, "It's still early."

Catfish started again on April 23, had no decision, and we lost 11–7 to Boston, dropping into last place. Bonds wasn't hitting, and Hunter was getting frustrated now. Not until

his next start, April 27, did he finally win, beating Milwaukee 10–1 at home. It lifted us out of last place, took a lot
of heat off Hunter, and seemed to straighten us out.

I had helped break some of the tension on Catfish in that
game when a foul ball was lifted back near our dugout and
I chased it, only to have it fall into the seats. But seated
right there in the first row was one of the best-looking girls
I'd ever seen at a baseball game.

So I went back to the plate, called time, and went out to
the mound to visit Hunter. "Cat," I said, "see if you can
throw another pop-up right there again."

I was feeling better now physically, and was off to a super
start at bat. By early May, I was hitting over .350, and from
May 4 to May 25, I led the American League in hitting. I
felt I had really come back, and that we'd get our act
together and win the pennant. It turned out to be wishful
thinking.

We started to play good ball in June, opening the month
with an eight-game winning streak and taking five more in
the third week. On June 24, we moved into first place, spent
four of the next five days there, and then dropped back to
second. We were never on top again.

Hunter had straightened himself out and was on the way
to one of the best seasons a Yankee pitcher had ever enjoyed. He would pitch a complete game almost every time
he was on the mound, and wound up with 328 innings and
thirty complete games, the highest Yankee totals in half a
century. He won twenty-three games—it was the fifth consecutive season in which he'd pass twenty—joining Walter
Johnson and Lefty Grove as the only American Leaguers to
make this tremendous achievement.

But the other half of our new dynamic duo did not enjoy
the same total success. Bobby Bonds, who started slowly,
got his bat going in May and was really leading the charge.
He was doing it all—at bat, in the field, and on the bases.
For a few weeks, he was everything he'd been advertised to

be, and we felt we were watching the league's Most Valuable Player in the making.

But on the night of June 7 in Chicago, Bobby misplayed a fly ball over his head and hit the right field wall. He came crashing down and badly injured his knee. It was the first serious injury of his career, and it was enough to devastate our offense.

On June 13, Elliott Maddox wrecked his knee on the wet outfield at Shea Stadium, and we lost him for the season. He had been hitting .307, getting on base, and playing a brilliant center field.

On July 12, Ron Blomberg tore his shoulder, and we lost him for two and a half years. Poor Ronnie. Few men could mash right-hand pitching as he could—every pitch was a solid line drive down the line. But he never could master left-hand pitching. Even in the minors, if he'd play against lefties, it would set him back against right-handers. And he just wasn't very good defensively or as a base runner. So as talented as he was, he lacked the complete skills to be a great star. But we'd really miss his bat.

Lou Piniella, who'd led the club in hitting the year before, developed a strange inner ear problem which required surgery. He didn't feel right all year, and wound up hitting an embarrassing .196 with no home runs.

Bonds wasn't out long, but he just wasn't the same when he came back. Whereas he'd been carrying us while he was hot, the momentum was gone, and for the rest of the season, he'd be just another bat in the lineup, good some days, not so good on others.

The fans finally voted me to the starting All-Star team in 1975, but a little bit of the honor was missing because Fisk was injured. He'd been hurt early enough not to run away with the election—in past years, he'd waited until late May or June to get hurt. I always said he might be a great player, particularly in Fenway Park, if he could ever play a full season without getting hurt. But he'd always manage to injure himself, and all people could say was "imagine what a year he could have had." Well, he proved he could be a good player when he played injury-free in 1977, but until that time, he was always grabbing credit for things I'd already accomplished.

A few weeks after the All-Star Game, on July 29, my son Mike was born. He was a little squatty, but he didn't have a moustache and showed no signs of being grouchy, so I knew he'd be okay. I love watching the kids grow. Tracy and Kelly were old enough now to help Diana be a mother to Mike, and I just thought I'd been blessed with one of the all-time great families.

We lost three out of four to Boston in late July, and the pressure began to build on Bill Virdon as we sank further back in the games-behind column. Although Steinbrenner was never on the scene, we could almost feel his presence with each loss. We were ten out as August arrived, and the rumors were flying. They went rampant when Billy Martin was fired by the Texas Rangers.

On August 1, Catfish beat the Indians 5–4, with Fred Stanley making a great catch for the final out. But when we got to the clubhouse, the TV lights were all packed into Virdon's little office, and the microphones were all waiting for him.

"Have you been fired, Bill?" they asked.

"I haven't been told anything," he answered. And he hadn't, I'm sure, or he would have said so, because one thing you can count on is Bill's honesty.

"The rumors are all over the city," the reporters persisted. "Gabe Paul's been out of town the last few days. What's going on?"

"I have no idea," Bill kept saying, the pressure building on him. And seeing all the extra reporters on the scene, we knew something had to be up.

After the reporters had departed, Bill's phone rang. I'm

sure he knew who it was before he picked it up. It was Gabe
Paul, asking him to come across the street to the Yankee
offices when he was dressed. And that was the last we saw
of Bill Virdon.

As we drove to the ball park the next day, Old Timers'
Day, the radio reported the Yankees had called a press conference for noon, and that Billy Martin was in town. So we
knew Martin was our new manager.

I didn't know Billy personally, but I knew he was a fine
manager. He won division championships in Minnesota
and Detroit, and then he took a bad Texas club and made it
a good one. But in every case, he'd gotten fired in disputes
with the front office. His most recent firing had been only
several days earlier.

The day was chaotic, what with the 1975 Yankees, all the
old-timers and a million reporters, all jammed into the little clubhouse for the festivities and the press conference. It
was maddening. Just getting out into the fresh air gave us
the energy we needed to win, and we made Billy's debut a
success, beating Cleveland 5–3.

The next day, when things began to calm down, Billy had
a chance to talk to each of us individually. It was not a particularly pleasant meeting for Elliott Maddox and Jim Mason, neither of whom had gotten along with Billy in Texas.
Maddox, in fact, had played for Billy in Detroit, and hadn't
gotten along with him there. But promises were made all
around that things would be fine.

I speak my mind on occasions such as this, and didn't hesitate for a minute to tell Billy some of my concerns.

"I call my own pitches," I told him. "I've studied these hitters for a long time, and I know what I'm doing behind the
plate. I know you like to call pitches sometimes, but frankly, I don't think you're as qualified as I am. Give me a few
days to show you, and you'll see I'm right."

He gave me the opportunity, and I responded well. We

won six of the first eight games Billy managed, and to this day, I call all my own pitches. I respect the man for giving me the chance and letting me prove my point.

I remember the first time Billy came to the mound as Yankee manager. Rudy May was the pitcher, and he was struggling a little, so I went out to talk to him. And out of the corner of my eye, I saw Billy trotting out, too.

When he arrived at the mound, I looked at him and half-seriously snarled, "What the hell are you doin' here?"

Amazingly, Billy turned right around and went back to the dugout. He never said a word. We kid about it to this day.

Unfortunately, we couldn't sustain that early winning streak under Martin, and we remained locked into third place for the rest of the season. We played a little better baseball, particularly Sandy Alomar at second, but we were too late to catch Boston. Still, the Yankees didn't change managers to win the 1975 pennant. They changed because Billy Martin was available, and he was worth the change at any time.

Despite his injury, Bonds hit his thirty home runs and stole his thirty bases. He was really satisfied when he reached the thirty homer mark near the end of the season, having played in pain. He had reason to be proud, and we all shared the satisfaction he felt. Sure it was disappointing to finish twelve games out of first. But considering the devastating injuries we received, we could hardly have expected better.

I had a great season—hit safely in 117 of the 157 games in which I played, including fifty-six games with two or more hits. I had 190 hits for the year, hit .318, drove in 102 runs, and won my third Gold Glove award. I'd have loved to help us make it into the playoffs, but it was not to be.

It had been a crazy season in a lot of little ways. Back in July, umpire Art Frantz ruled me out for using an "illegal" bat after I'd singled and driven in a run. The bat was illegal, he said, because the pine tar was too high up on the handle.

A couple of weeks later, another umpire noticed the same thing and just told me to wipe it off.

I charged the mound that year in Baltimore, after the Oriole pitcher had thrown a few pitches too close to me. The pitcher? Mike Torrez, later a teammate. It was just one of those things that happen in baseball, and we never maintained any bad feelings over it.

At the end of the season, I grew a beard. I never told anyone why—just for the general amusement of it—and no one made as big a deal out of it as they did when I grew another one a couple of years later.

ON THE ROAD: THE SAGA OF A SEASON

Ballplayers live in an unreal world. Those who recognize this make the best of it and deal with it appropriately. Others get so swept up in it they lose a sense of reality.

The hardest part of baseball for me is the road. Nothing seems normal when you travel with a baseball team. The hours, the meals, the living conditions—you tend to lose all conception of normal human behavior.

We ordinarily begin a road trip right after the final game of a homestand, often on Sunday. About an hour and a half after the game is over, we emerge from the overheated clubhouse and board an overcrowded bus for the airport. The day's game is still on our minds. If we've lost it, the bus is relatively silent. If we've won, spirits are higher.

The manager sits up front unless he's got a separate ride to the airport. Also in the front are the writers—about five—the broadcasters, a radio engineer, a TV producer, two trainers, the traveling secretary, a public relations man, and the coaches. That usually means the players sit in the back half of the bus. If the trip to the airport is long enough, a card game will probably get started. If not, the cards will wait until we board the plane.

A lot of players carry portable tape decks, each blaring a different kind of music. It used to get on Bill Virdon's nerves, but he wouldn't say anything. Our garment bags hanging from the rails on the ceiling swing to the motion of the bus. Ellie Howard has traveled with the same bag since the beginning of time.

We're required to wear ties and jackets when we travel, but sometimes the color coordination is pretty weak, and we look a little ridiculous. Particularly at the end of a trip when we throw together whatever is left. I've never been considered a good dresser, but by the final day of a two-week road trip, I look as good, or as bad, as anyone else.

If we've got some crazy personalities aboard, it can make the trip very pleasant—very funny, in fact. Lou Piniella both gives and takes a tremendous amount of kidding. He and Mickey Rivers are super to have on a club.

Mickey got off one of the best lines I ever heard when Reggie Jackson was picking on him early in 1977. While Reggie was having his troubles at the plate, he was full of talk about his 160 IQ. Rivers started speaking to him once, and Reggie cut him off with "I can't understand anything you say." Rivers came right back with "If you'd stop reading and start hitting, we'd all be a lot better off!"

With Dock Ellis, Oscar Gamble, Carlos May and Catfish all getting in on the act, we had some hilarious times together.

There are times when all the black players sit together and all the white players sit together. A stranger boarding the bus might think we're all members of the Ku Klux Klan and the Black Panthers, the way we go at it. I wouldn't even repeat some of the things we say to each other. I'd call Bobby Bonds "boy" constantly—I still do. And he'd call me a honkey right back and we'd go at each other.

The other players would pick up the "argument," until eventually someone would say something completely outrageous and unheard of, and the whole bus would break up. But the constant kidding relieves any tensions which might exist, and it makes it easier for a pack of twenty-five men to live together closely for seven months. By 1976, the team was half black and half white, so no one felt picked on. Or rather, everyone did.

The bus brings us up to the airport terminal and we parade through the airport to our gate. The team equipment and our baggage is all taken separately by truck from the ball park.

If it's a reasonable hour and the airport is crowded, we get stared at like a herd of circus animals. Obviously, as a traveling party of about fifty men, we raise eyebrows. People usually figure out that we're a sports team, but we usually walk by too fast for them to figure out who we are— unless they notice Yogi, one of America's most recognized people. We really can't stop to sign autographs without falling behind, so people sometimes think we're snobs.

We take commercial flights when they're available. But if we're flying, for instance, from Kansas City to Anaheim at midnight, we need a charter. If we've got a charter flight, which we do about half the time, then we can board easily. Card games are set up, and the players enjoy stretching out in the coach section. The manager, the coaches, a couple of players, and the writers like first class. It doesn't really matter, because we've all got plenty of room, and we all get the same service.

The commercial flights put us on planes with regular passengers, and most of them are displeased at our arrival. There are times when the game runs late and the plane is held up waiting for us. We always reserve the entire first class section, which causes bad feelings, and we sometimes cause a delay going through airport security, with all the stereo equipment and attaché cases. Still, the people want autographs once we're airborne—always for their "nephews or their grandchildren," never for themselves.

The planes are too noisy to get into any conversations, so we play cards, eat, have a beer, or sleep. I can get through the airline magazines in about ninety seconds.

Our pockets are full of meal money, which represents about $25 a day. It may sound like a lot, but if you've ever tried to eat three meals in a hotel, you know it doesn't go very far. Some of the lower-salaried players try to save a little meal money, but it's hardly worth it. They'd be lucky to save $20 on a two-week trip. In 1973, the Yankees released Johnny Callison late in August with a couple of days left on a road trip, and they deducted the remaining meal money from his travel check home. I'll never forget that.

When we land, we head straight for the main exit and hop on the bus, which is supposed to be waiting. It usually is, but I remember on our very first trip with Billy Martin, there was a mixup, and we walked into a deserted Cleveland Airport to find no bus. It took an hour just to find enough cabs to get us downtown—a very embarrassing hour for the traveling secretary.

When we get to the hotel, it's often well past midnight. There are usually three options available—go right to sleep and get the bags in the morning, wait in the lobby for the luggage to arrive by truck, or try to find an all-night diner for a snack. Finding a diner isn't always easy, and in a lot of cities, it's not really recommended.

The loneliness can start at this point. Everyone used to have roommates. Now, we're entitled to single rooms, and most people take them. It's you and the TV from then on, and the TV isn't designed for traveling ballplayers. Daytime television offers nothing of interest, and TV after midnight is pretty hopeless unless you catch a good late movie. We had one trip a few years ago, when we caught Phil Rizzuto's favorite movie, *North By Northwest*, in four different cities. We could read, but usually we just sleep, eat, and go to the ball park. We can't get involved in any recreational activities on the road, because of the risk of injury or just exhaustion.

It's frustrating when I call my wife and the kids are sick, or she misses me, or some crisis has arisen. There's nothing to do except talk to the kids on the phone and tell them I'll be home in a few days. I am missing a lot of their wonderful growing-up years. That's why I spend as much time with them as I can when we're home, or in the off-season.

A typical day starts with waking up around 11 A.M., assuming we've played a night game the night before. We wander down to breakfast in the hotel coffee shop; buy a newspaper, and study the box scores. We see what the local writers are saying about our opponent—who's hot, who's not.

Boston and Los Angeles have great sports sections. Chicago is good, too. New York could be good if as much space was devoted to reporting the games as to reporting the gossip.

I read the game stories and look over the box scores, and we'll talk among ourselves at breakfast about last night's games. "Did you see that Palmer got knocked out in the fourth?" "Can you believe Bowa hit another home run?" "How many in a row is that for the Royals?"

Afternoons are endless. If the weather is nice, we go shopping—not that we need anything, but it's something to do. Minneapolis is a nice walking town, with its beautiful downtown mall. Michigan Avenue in Chicago is nice, and Kansas City has a good downtown, but unfortunately we don't always stay downtown. The newer American League cities, Toronto and Seattle, are both quite attractive. I didn't expect Toronto to be as progressive in a business sense as it is.

We also play in towns where there's nothing to do at all. In Oakland, Arlington, Baltimore, Cleveland, Detroit, and Milwaukee, there is either nothing to see or no desire to see it. Milwaukee is a nice restaurant town, but not even restaurants are readily available to us. We don't want to eat out before a night game, because a big meal can make you loggy. And after a game, it's usually too late to have dinner in a nice place. So we take most meals quickly in the hotel restaurants.

I spend some of my afternoons on the phone with my business associates in Cleveland. Even when I'm at home, I spend a good deal of the day taking care of my business interests, working with figures, really taxing my thinking potential. That's why I enjoy getting to the park in the evening and letting my physical being free. It represents a good balance for me.

If we wait for the bus to go to the park, that's usually two hours before game time. Often, we'll hail cabs and go earlier just to unwind in the clubhouse, play some cards, relax on the training table, or do some early hitting. I've gone to the ball parks as early as six hours before game time just for lack of anything better to do. The companionship of the other players helps pass the time.

The best visiting clubhouses are in Anaheim and Kansas City. Both are roomy, well lit, and nicely air-conditioned. In the older ball parks, like Detroit and Chicago, we always feel as though we're stepping on people, and the ventilation could kill you.

Indoor baseball in Seattle doesn't really appeal to me. I suppose from a practical standpoint it would be better if all parks were domed, but I enjoy the fresh air. I don't mind artificial turf, however, so I can't be labeled a purist. It gives the fans a faster game and provides for truer bounces on the playing surface.

The games are what I enjoy most about the traveling. Once the game starts, it's just you against them. No hangers-on standing around the batting cage, no wasted hours waiting around. It's what the trip is all about, and I really love the competition. I don't know if I could ever stay in baseball if it meant sitting on the bench. The days are long enough without that burden.

It's impractical as well as expensive for wives to travel, even if no kids are involved. They aren't allowed on the charters, so we have to manage separate travel arrangements. And since we have to get to the park early, we have to leave our wives alone for as many as seven or eight hours. In a lot of American League cities, that's unthinkable.

So I do the best I can. I'm glad I have my business interests to keep my mind from going stale. The rest of the trip can be described as sleep, eat, walk, read, bus, practice, play, bus, sleep. Day after day. We finish a few days in one city, and we're off to the next. And the pattern keeps repeating.

Players are always faced with the problems of relocation. Very few are year-round residents of the cities in which they play. Among the Yankees in recent years, only Chambliss, White, Maddox and Blomberg lived near New York.

When spring training comes, players have to make a decision on what to do with the family. If the kids are in school, do you leave them there, or do you transfer them to a temporary school in Florida for a few weeks? It's unsettling if you do, but it's a long time to be without them if you don't.

The team doesn't require us to live in the club's spring training hotel, but if we do, only our own way is paid, and it's expensive to have the family living in a hotel for up to six weeks—also inconvenient, because our wives can't cook for the kids. Most players rent apartments or homes for the six weeks—not an easy assignment. Then, as spring training is winding down, assuming a player knows he'll make the club, he has to think about a place to live in the team's city. Should he live in a hotel until school lets out in June and then rent a home?

It's not easy to rent a furnished home for just the summer, particularly in the same area where other guys are living—this makes car pooling easier, for the players and for the wives.

For a few years, I owned a home in New Jersey, but eventually I became dissatisfied with living there, and longed to settle back in Canton. In other years, I rented places, but we always felt transient.

Then, as the season winds down, we have to think about travel plans back home. Who drives the car? Who packs up the house? What about getting the kids back into school?

There is a certain sameness to the baseball life that, after the passage of years, tarnishes the glitter. But no discussion of the game could be complete without mention of the glamour as well.

People are always eager to do things for us, get things for us, take care of our needs. There are times when we do take advantage of these situations. You never lose the thrill of seeing your picture on a baseball card. Or even seeing your name and picture in the newspaper—except when it's insulting or embarrassing. The adulation of the fans feels terrific—don't let anyone say it doesn't. New York fans have always been great to me, and I think I've given them a lot in return.

The pay is now super—who's kidding whom? But, of course, we're only talking about a small percentage of a man's earning years. It behooves a player to earn and invest as much as he can when he can, before the years have passed him by and he finds his salary starting all over again at the bottom of another profession.

That's why I'm so proud of the security I've been able to develop for my family. The day won't come when I'm starting out at the bottom. I've been fortunate, through my real estate interests, to carve out a separate and lucrative profession which will carry me well after I've given up baseball.

I don't look to give advice, but when players ask me about

my business interests, I tell them it's my real estate investments that made me able to maximize the profits from my
baseball career. I have worked the real estate and the baseball earnings into a package which brings me a maximum
return financially, and which will take care of Thurman,
Diana, Tracy, Kelly and Mike long after I've left baseball.
No magic was involved. I just took the time to learn what I
was doing, developed trust in the right people, and set up
for myself a financial situation which years ago I would
never have dreamed possible. It's kept my mind active and
made me a better overall person.

I like to think that I'm multidimensional—not just a
dumb jock who can talk only sports. I pride myself on being
able to discuss anything with anybody. It's not necessary to
waste away your entire baseball life, giving no thought to
the future. There's plenty of time during a baseball season
to keep the mind active and get involved in other projects.
A baseball player may live in an unreal world, but if you
can keep your hand in the real world at the same time,
you'll be a lot better off for the experience when you emerge
from the clubhouse for the last time.

FREE AGENCY ARRIVES

The 1976 season didn't promise to proceed any more smoothly than the 1975 season. In a move just as shocking as the Murcer trade a year earlier, the Yankees, during the winter meetings of 1975, sent Bobby Bonds to California in exchange for Mickey Rivers and Ed Figueroa. The next day, George Medich was traded to Pittsburgh for Dock Ellis, Ken Brett, and Willie Randolph. The meetings had been going along rather slowly until Gabe Paul started the ball rolling, and by the time the week was over, more players had been traded than ever before.

I knew the Medich deal was a good one right away. Randolph was the key man there, although he was virtually unknown, having only played a couple of months in the majors. But we had seen him the previous spring when we played the Pirates in San Juan, and we knew this guy had something. We call Willie "Mr. Personality," because he's always so sullen and silent, but he sure can play second base.

Dock Ellis won seventeen games for us after a lot of people had written him off. Dock is an amazing character—a

125

lot of fun once you get to know him. I could see how he might have gotten on people's nerves in the past, but he played a big role in keeping the team loose. And when he and Steinbrenner ran into salary hassles a year later, off he went to Oakland for Mike Torrez, another seventeen-game winner and a big man in the playoffs and the World Series for us.

Brett didn't have much of a place on our pitching staff, so Gabe sent him to Chicago for Carlos May, our top designated hitter in 1976. With all these deals to his credit, Gabe continued to build quite a record in the trade market.

The Bonds trade, however, caught everyone by surprise, particularly Bobby. He had really given us a helluva season in 1975, playing hurt for more than half the year, and we had figured on having Bonds around for many years. I didn't know what to make of that trade at first. We gave up a lot of power in dealing him, and it didn't seem to leave us with any consistent long ball threat, especially from the right-hand side.

It was just one of those deals that depended on what kinds of years the principals had. A wait-and-see deal. Rivers, being perhaps the fastest man in baseball, brought a new dimension to our attack. But on that alone, we weren't going anywhere. After all, he'd played the same role with the Angels, and they hadn't done well at all. Figueroa was coming off a fine season, one in which he'd started in the minors and wound up with sixteen wins in the majors. But that was his only track record to date, so I took a wait-and-see attitude too.

Baseball's infamous reserve clause was much in the news that winter. Although Curt Flood had lost his fight against it in the Supreme Court a few years earlier, the Court had brought attention to this denial of a player's freedom of choice. It's a shame Curt wasn't still active in 1976 and in a position to reap the benefits of the final act on the "bondage," as he called it.

The reserve clause was the statement in the player's contract which tied him to the club for life. Only by drawing a release at the end of a career was a player technically free. Joe DiMaggio, who retired in 1951, was still "property of the New York Yankees," as were Mickey Mantle, Bobby Richardson, Tony Kubek, and anyone else who ever voluntarily retired.

When the free agent draft was instituted in 1965, a player's movement had been even further restricted. If you were drafted by a club, you eventually had to sign with that club—or with a club in a later draft—and then you were bound to that team forever. In no other profession could a man be prevented from seeking the best deal for himself.

After the Flood case, Ted Simmons of the Cardinals had threatened to test the reserve clause by failing to sign for much of the season. And my own teammate, Sparky Lyle, came very close to being the first man to play without signing a contract for a full year, then declaring himself a free agent after the season—only a last-minute signing for two years prevented it.

Then Andy Messersmith of the Dodgers and Dave McNally of the Expos went through the entire 1975 season unsigned, and announced they were not "reserved" for the 1976 season. They were considering themselves free agents. The matter was sent to a professional arbitrator, Peter Seitz, the man who had ruled on Hunter's free agency the year before.

The Hunter affair had given everyone a pretty good idea of the market value for players if general free agency came about. Certainly, I had as good an idea of my value to the Yankees as anyone did. It was a value determined not only by what I could do for the Yankees, but also by what I could do by *not* playing for an opponent.

Because I hadn't signed my 1976 contract by the time spring training opened, I was "renewed," as was the practice, and my salary was cut twenty percent, the legal maximum a team is permitted.

Bowie Kuhn had by this time lifted George Steinbrenner's suspension for "good behavior," so he was back in full swing. One day, I was on the field in Fort Lauderdale when George came over and said, "Hi, Thurman."

"Hi?" I said. "You're talking to me like a friend—you're no friend of mine. You cut my salary twenty percent a year after I'd gotten only a $5,000 raise."

The previous December, when negotiations had begun between myself and Gabe Paul, I asked for a three-year contract. Multiyear contracts were still quite unusual, but I'm a man who likes to put my affairs in order. I was happy with the Yankees, felt they'd always been good to me, and I was prepared to give away my potential free agency in exchange for the security of a three-year contract. I sought $120,000 for 1976, with $10,000 raises for each of the next two years.

Of course, the Messersmith-McNally case had yet to be decided, and so Gabe Paul was not interested in my proposal at that time. And Steinbrenner later told me, "You're going to be surprised with the Messersmith case—it's not going to be decided the way the players want."

Well, I held onto my offer, and the Yankees held onto their refusal, so I said, "Fine, then trade me to Cleveland."

Players sometimes laugh when I talk about playing for Cleveland, which is not considered one of the glamour franchises. And although the city itself is not as attractive as some, the suburban areas are quite nice, and Canton, where we were constructing a beautiful new house, is only forty-five miles away. It's of course not only my home, but my wife's home, our parents home, and the birthplace of our three children. I have all of my business interests in Ohio, and I'd be able to follow them much more carefully if I was home all year.

Given all of those factors, Cleveland was an attractive place for me to play ball. I don't need to play in a glamour city. I don't seek the publicity, and, in fact, haven't received it. I care about my family, I care about my business interests, which provide security for my family, and I care about getting a good and honest contract from my baseball employer.

The Yankees and I remained at an impasse as spring training proceeded. Then came the decision on Messersmith and McNally—the players had won. The practice of playing out one's option had prevailed, in the judgment of the arbitrator. The club owners, in a touch of good sportsmanship, immediately fired Peter Seitz, the arbitrator.

Now Steinbrenner invited me to his Florida hotel room. "You want the $120,000, $130,000, $140,000 for three years?" he said. "Okay, you've got it."

"Well, wait a minute, George," I answered. "That was then, and this is now."

The Messersmith-McNally case had opened up new avenues for baseball players. A few weeks earlier, I had been prepared to gamble away the ruling in exchange for the contract. Now that the ruling had been made, I would not have been a very good businessman to accept the offer, in view of what I had to gain by being a free agent after the season. And George Steinbrenner, not a bad businessman himself, certainly recognized that.

My twenty-percent cut was restored to bring good faith back into play as we continued to talk. Meanwhile, the Yankees continued to put themselves in the forefront of generous salary payments by jumping on the Messersmith bandwagon and seeking to sign him. In fact, midway through spring training, the Yankees announced they *had* signed Andy—the pitching staff would now be the finest in the game.

But like many things in the never-ending controversy of the Yankees, the Messersmith signing never came to be. Disagreements with Andy's agent, misunderstandings all around, and perhaps a premature announcement of the deal killed it all, and we lost him.

In early March, I met again with Steinbrenner, and he

was in a more giving mood. I told him of my feelings regarding the new free agent rules and of my interest in staying with the Yankees if I could get a contract making it worth my giving up free agency. He said he couldn't arrange that, and I said, "Fine, I'll play out my option and be a free agent."

I wasn't looking to hold him up. If I were a free agent coming from another club, he'd certainly have met my price—he proved that with the money he paid later on to others. I was just looking to get my worth, and I was in a position to determine my worth.

Two weeks later, on March 24, we met again. Now he agreed that I would be the highest-salaried player on the team. Furthermore, he said he really wanted a pennant very badly, and he'd make it worth my while to help bring that about. He told me he'd give me the right to renegotiate my contract if we won the 1976 pennant.

I signed that day, and became the sixth Yankee in history—joining DiMaggio, Mantle, Murcer, Bonds, and Hunter—to earn $100,000 in one season. I had no reason to doubt anything that was said in negotiations with George, because he'd never given me any reason for doubting him.

If we didn't have an employer-employee relationship, George and I might be the best of friends. In many ways, we're a lot alike. We're both hustlers, really go-getters. We like being involved in a lot of different things, we both play to win, and we both like making money.

George is a lot of fun and a real charmer among his friends. He's done very noble and charitable things for many people over the years. And, of course, he's done a wonderful job in building up the Yankees, in bringing a winner to New York after so many years. There's a lot about the man I respect and admire. But I'm afraid we were to have our troubles down the road over the next couple of years.

My signing was the least of the newsworthy events dur-

ing spring training of 1976. And while the Messersmith
affair was significant, the major story had been the opening
of the camps themselves.

Because of the confusion surrounding the new Basic
Agreement, the owners decided not to open camps. Their
reasoning was based on the events of the players' strike of
1972, which occurred after the spring training games. That
strike had made training camp practically useless, and the
owners were not about to let themselves in for a repeat performance. The camps remained closed, and informal workouts were conducted all over the country until Commissioner Kuhn ordered them open.

No one liked the idea of closing the camps, particularly
not the fans, and it was an unpleasant event, to be sure.
But the resulting Basic Agreement was a strong one for the
players, and, fortunately, no strike was necessary to help
bring it about. Those of us who were around for the '72
strike still had some sad feelings over the necessity of it,
but time heals, and the fans tended to forget it. I'm glad we
didn't have to stir up old memories by a similar action in
1976.

When the camps opened and Steinbrenner returned, the
next newsworthy event was the arrival of Oscar Gamble
from the Indians. Oscar, while playing for the Indians, had
worn his hair in the biggest Afro in the sports world. Although the Yankees' haircut policy was a little relaxed during George's suspension, his return meant a toughening of
the rules.

Word reached Oscar before the first workout. "Get it cut,
or you can't work out." Now, Oscar could have caused trouble by refusing to get it cut and lodging a formal grievance.
I doubt the Yankees could have won a hearing, trying to
deny the man a basic individual right which caused no
harm to anyone.

But after just a few hours, Oscar gave in and had his hair
cut. The before and after pictures ran all over the country,

and the Yankees were saved a great deal of embarrassment. It certainly would have been interesting to see what
would have happened had Oscar refused to comply. I know
Billy Martin was in no hurry to get in the middle of that
one.

This was Billy's first spring training with the club, and
he'd talked a good deal about his well-run training program
and how he could mold the club to get them ready to go
from the start. Unfortunately, the delay in opening the
camps forced him to hurry us into shape and made it almost
impossible for any dark horse to make the club.

I don't think there had been any love lost between the
Yankees and the Mets during our tenure in Shea Stadium.
It was something like having relatives move in for two
years—you try to be accommodating, but eventually, you
feel crowded. Everyone was as happy as could be about returning to Yankee Stadium.

Everyone, of course, except the New York taxpayers, or a
lot of them, anyway. The Yankee Stadium modernization
was originally scheduled to cost $24 million, a figure used
for budgetary reasons to get the project rolling. But costs
skyrocketed, and eventually, the tab was well over $50 mil-
lion, with the surrounding roadways and parking areas
raising it closer to $100 million. The press liked the ring of
the latter figure and used it all the time.

Steinbrenner was taking a lot of heat about the new Stadium when, in fact, he had inherited the project from the
previous owners. He was forced into the position of defending the expenditure, which he'd had no part in.

To his credit, Steinbrenner endured a lot that spring. He
was back in full force, but everyone who interviewed him
wanted to know about Watergate and his suspension, and
he was anxious to put that behind him. The stadium modernization was controversial, the Bonds trade was controversial, my salary hassle was making news, the Gamble
haircut had made long hair a big deal again, and the uncer-

tainty over the new free agent rules and the Basic Agreement were creating questions about the whole structure of the game.

It was a couple of weeks before camp ended that I was named captain of the team, which, as I said, didn't mean as much to me then as it did later. I felt it was in George's interest to have a captain to give *his* team a classier look. It was, I felt, a move designed for his ego more than mine.

On top of all of this, as we were just wrapping things up and preparing to head home, I broke my finger. It was just a freak accident, catching a foul ball, but it sure as hell was broken. I couldn't believe my bad luck.

For a few days, the Yankees announced only that the finger was "sprained," attempting to make a deal for another front line catcher just in case. An announcement of the break would have made it all the more difficult to swing a deal, with the other teams knowing they were desperate. Poor Rick Dempsey had to catch every inning of every exhibition game for about a week, knowing that it was only until I got back or until the Yankees could make another deal.

The press couldn't be fooled, however, and it was in the papers before long that the finger was broken. But I was determined not to let a foolish and freak accident spoil the new season for me, and I told Billy I'd be ready by opening day. I don't know if he believed me, but I sure intended to be.

We wound up training camp with a 10–7 record and a pretty set lineup, featuring Chambliss, Randolph, Stanley, and Nettles in the infield, White, Rivers, and Gamble in the outfield, Dempsey catching until I got well, Piniella (or Gamble) as the designated hitter, and a starting rotation of Hunter, Figueroa, Ellis, and Rudy May, with Lyle and Tidrow in the bullpen. We didn't look bad at all.

A NEW STADIUM

We opened the 1976 season in the cold weather that is typical of Milwaukee in early April. On days like that, I agree
with the fans who say the season is too long—it starts too
early and ends too late. It's terrible to play in such cold
weather. You can scarcely grip the baseball.

I could hardly hold the bat, but that didn't have much to
do with the cold. I was the designated hitter in our opening-
day lineup, with Dempsey catching, and my finger still broken. I was beginning to have doubts about being able to
play in the home opener a week later.

Our start was not much to speak of. Jim Slaton beat us
5–0, with Catfish absorbing the shutout. We hoped the Cat
wouldn't have the same problems getting his first win as he
had the year before. Hunter complained that the mound
wasn't right in Milwaukee, and in fact Billy protested the
game over it. We didn't win the protest, of course, but it
marked the start of a year in which we didn't take many
losses easily.

There are subtle variations in the field and equipment
which only people who play baseball 150 or more times a

year can feel. A mound can be just a shade off in terms of
the slope. An infield can be just a touch too soft. Even baseballs, which are hand-stitched, can vary from one to another, and pitchers can feel the differences immediately.
That's why you see pitchers ask for new baseballs from
time to time.

If the mound worked against us on opening day, someone
was looking after us the next day to make up for it. I doubt
I'll ever play in another game quite like it.

We had a 9–7 lead in the last of the ninth inning, when
the Brewers loaded the bases. Dave Pagan, a hard-throwing but wild and nervous right-hander came in for us, and
he faced Don Money. Money swung and sent the ball sail-
ing over the fence for a grand-slam home run. We had practically won the game, and with one swing, it looked as
though we'd blown it.

But it didn't quite work out that way. Chris Chambliss at
first had called time before the pitch, and the umpire had
granted it. Everyone else missed it, and the pitch was
made, but when Chambliss hollered that time had been
called, the umpires had to agree. Money was called back,
Ken Brett came in to save the game, and we held on to win.
I don't have to tell you what kind of argument followed that
one.

So the pattern for the season was set. We had played two
games, lost over a bad mound, and won over a recalled homer. It was going to be some kind of year.

I remained the designated hitter as we moved on to Baltimore, where Catfish beat Ross Grimsley 3–0 on national
TV, and then Dock Ellis beat Jim Palmer 7–1 to put us in
first place. Now it was time to try out the newest park in
the league, our own.

We had a workout in Yankee Stadium the day before the
opener. Everybody was impressed with the way the place
had shaped up. The clubhouse couldn't be nicer, with large
lockers, thick carpeting, a big trainer's room, a comfortable

lounge, and plenty of space to move around. Unlike Shea, it could be a relaxing place before a game.

Billy's office didn't have a carpet, which was his first complaint. The dugouts weren't built just right either—you couldn't see the field from the bench. We all had to sit propped up against the wall with our feet on the bench. Electrical outlets had been installed every six feet along the back wall of the dugout, and I'm still trying to figure out what they're for. The helmet rack was built on the near side of the dugout, which meant after each at bat we had to fling our helmets across the front of the dugout for the batboy. It made us look as though we were mad everytime we were out.

Of course, the fans were much more comfortable, and everyone agreed the place was beautiful. But what most appealed to me was the shorter dimensions of left field. It would now be possible, although still not easy, to hit a ball with good authority and see it clear the fence. In the old stadium, many of my best shots were just long outs.

It was obvious in batting practice that the ball was going to carry real well in the new stadium. Everyone was zinging them into the seats. Perhaps the new scoreboard, which served as a barrier to outfield wind currents, caused this.

My finger was just about healed, and I was happy to report that I'd be able to catch on opening day.

The opening-day ceremonies were memorable. The program was like a mini-Old Timers Day, except the guests weren't all baseball people. People who had starred at Yankee Stadium in different sports were invited back—to celebrate our opener. Joe Louis, Frank Gifford, Kyle Rote—and, of course, all the baseball legends were there. DiMaggio, Mantle, Ford, Mrs. Babe Ruth, Mrs. Lou Gehrig.

Rudy May was our starting pitcher, but the Dude didn't have it, and Dan Ford of Minnesota touched him for a first-inning home run, the first ever in the new park. Since Babe Ruth had hit the first in the "old" stadium, Ford's homer

was considered to be of historic significance. Then I hit the
first home run for the Yankees, and the second in the new
stadium. So I just missed out on "immortality."

The amazing thing about both of our homers was that
they were hit into the new bullpen in left field. It was a re-
duced distance, compared to the old stadium, but still quite
a shot. Incredibly, not another ball was hit there, by anyone, all season.

We beat the Twins 11–4 for our fourth straight victory.
With the opener behind us, we felt as though we were ready
to run up a pretty good streak. It's hard to develop much
momentum in baseball, because there's always some pitcher waiting for you with great stuff, and good pitching will
usually stop good hitting. But after only four games, we
were feeling like a pretty decent team. And when Ed Figueroa shut out the Twins 10–0, running the streak to five
straight, we knew we were onto something good.

The next week, we had to go to West Point for an exhibition game against the Army baseball team. One year, we
had four exhibitions during the season—with the Mets,
West Point, Syracuse, and the International League All-
Stars. Even one a year is a lot, considering how few off-days
there are in a season. I know each is for a good cause, but
there are times you wish the club would just donate the
money and avoid the inconvenience of playing a game. As it
is, the fans never get to see the regulars anyway, unless it's
just for a swing or two.

By the beginning of May, things were definitely going
our way. We returned to Yankee Stadium ready to meet the
Orioles for a three-game series. Catfish was scheduled to
pitch the opener on Friday night.

When you're a regular starting pitcher, you always have
a fairly good idea of when you're scheduled to work, and
therefore, when you can schedule other things. Hunter
made arrangements to have a television commercial for a
chewing tobacco filmed, and because you can't plan those

things on one or two days' notice, he had committed himself to May 14 for the shooting. Catfish figured if he wasn't doing the commercial he'd be home working around the house before the game. And since he approaches everything in an easygoing style, he didn't consider that it might be taxing on him to stand outside in uniform for a few hours filming a commercial on the day he was pitching.

Well, if George Steinbrenner hadn't been in town that day, and if Catfish had beat the Orioles that night, we might never have heard another word. But George was there, and he looked down from his stadium office and saw about 100 technicians all over the field, with Hunter right in the middle of the mob scene. He ordered a quick wrapup to the filming. Hunter gave up four runs in the first inning that night, including a two-run homer by Reggie Jackson. We had a feeling we'd all hear about it.

The next day, a memo came to each player, informing us in so many words that outside activities were "out" during the season. It seemed to imply speaking engagements, commercials, and the like, and we all got on Cat pretty good for having caused our new restrictions. But, of course, no one took it very seriously, despite the lesson Hunter taught us right before our eyes.

We kept winning, and by the middle of May, we were seriously considered the team to beat in the American League East. Mickey Rivers was having a great season, and Willie Randolph was everything he had been built up to be. The Bonds trade was looking good after all, and the right-hand power wasn't so noticeably absent.

A few days after the Orioles series, the Red Sox came to town. With them the defending champs, and us in first place, it was obviously a big series, both for the fans and for the players. The adrenaline really flows whenever these two teams get together.

The action got heavy right in the first game. We were down 2–1 in the last of the sixth when Piniella and Fisk crashed together in a hard play at the plate. Immediately, both benches cleared, and a real free-for-all broke loose. Bill Lee, the Boston pitcher, should have known better than to get involved—he injured his shoulder in the scuffle and missed a couple of months.

When I'm in a baseball fight, I'll be as scrappy as anyone out there. But usually, everyone who runs out sort of stands around or tries to break things up. When I looked at the newspaper photos of that fight the next day, I saw Lee, Nettles, Rivers, Darrell Johnson and some others in the middle. I couldn't find myself, but I know I was in there.

We lost that game 8–2, but won a wild one 6–5 in twelve innings the next day, when Kerry Dineen, in his first at-bat after being called up from Syracuse, got the winning hit.

On Saturday, Catfish was at his finest, stopping Boston 1–0 on three hits. But on Sunday, we lost 7–6 before 53,000 people. Now we were three games ahead of the Orioles, and Boston was six back.

As mid-June approached, we still held a comfortable lead. Nettles, as always, had gotten over his early-season slump and was driving in a lot of runs. Oscar Gamble—just as strong without his Afro as he had been with it—was delivering a lot of big homers. And I was having a very steady season, getting a hit or two every day, driving in five or six runs a week, and throwing well.

We played the Mayor's Trophy Game against the Mets on June 14, with me in center field. It was certainly a lot more relaxing in the outfield than behind the plate, but I like the pitch-by-pitch involvement I have as a catcher, and I found my mind wandering out there.

Now it was June 15, the day known by all baseball players as the trading deadline, the last day in which you can make deals other than waiver deals within your own league. Even though we were in first place, we knew of Gabe Paul's long record in baseball, and he wouldn't miss a chance to pull off a big one if he could.

And he did. Two of them, in fact, the second one becoming historically significant.

In the first deal, we traded Rudy May, Tippy Martinez, Dave Pagan, Scott McGregor, and Rick Dempsey to the Orioles for Ken Holtzman, Doyle Alexander, Grant Jackson, Elrod Hendricks, and a minor league pitcher.

We seldom see ten men traded at once, and it's even more unusual to see two teams fighting for the pennant in the same division, dealing with each other.

And within hours of that deal, the Yankees bought Vida Blue from Oakland for $1.5 million.

Getting Vida Blue just seemed too good to be true. Charlie Finley, knowing he was on the verge of losing many of his fine players who hadn't signed 1976 contracts, made the only move he felt he could make—he sold Blue to us and Rollie Fingers and Joe Rudi to Boston for $1 million each. As he would later claim, he intended to use his new wealth to restock his team with free agents after the season.

Fingers and Rudi actually reported to the Red Sox and were in uniform. Blue never made it to our club. Within forty-eight hours, Commissioner Kuhn stopped the deals, claiming they were not in the best interests of baseball. As he saw it, disassembling a good team like Oakland in midseason and restocking rich teams involved in a pennant race was against the order of the system. Of course, the system was changing, and perhaps this was one price the game would have to pay for the freedom of the players.

By the end of the week, Kuhn ordered Blue, Rudi, and Fingers to return to Oakland. Eventually, Finley sued Kuhn, and many felt he was destined to win. But Kuhn was able to convince the court that the power to veto player transactions was in fact invested in the commissioner, and he won the case. After years of Marvin Miller being acknowledged as the most powerful man in baseball, Kuhn suddenly emerged with perhaps more power than any previous commissioner had ever exercised.

The Yankees proceeded to win seven in a row after the trading deadline, increasing our lead to eight games. So the loss of Blue wasn't so devastating. Even Steinbrenner, who could usually be counted on to yell and scream over such things, was surprisingly quiet about the decision in Kuhn's favor. Despite threats, the Yankees never filed a lawsuit. Vida Blue soon faded into memory as a Yankee who never was.

Ken Holtzman's arrival was important to me, as it developed. Not too long after he became a Yankee, he signed a five-year contract with the club. This would put him in a Yankee uniform until he was thirty-four years old. His pay was guaranteed, and he couldn't be traded without his permission. Within a year, everyone was wondering how the Yankees could have given him such a deal and then used him so little. Even Ken thought it was ridiculous.

Ken's new contract made him the highest-salaried player on the club, an honor Steinbrenner had promised would remain with me.

Sure enough, George called me up to his office after the Holtzman signing and gave me a raise. It was proof to me that he was a man of his word, and served to officially validate our agreement.

One more interesting event during the first half of the season: A new phenomenon had entered our league, and his name was Fidrych. Mark Fidrych of the Tigers. Not even part of the Tigers' roster in spring training, he had made the team, worked his way to the starting rotation, and become a household word by the time he beat us 5–1 in Detroit on June 28, for his eighth win in nine decisions.

Fidrych is no fool—he's a great self-promoter. But I felt some of his behavior was childish and bush, and I had said so. Before the game, Fidrych was talking about pitching to the Yankees, and when a reporter asked him about me, Mark said, "Who's Thurman Munson?" It was interesting to see how much reaction came from that. The reaction indicated that I was a figure to be reckoned with. As for him, more power to him!

Late in June I began to get banged up a little bit. I developed a staph infection from a spike wound in my right hand, and a little later hurt my right knee in a play at the plate with Charlie Spikes of Cleveland. Although I was happy when I found out I'd been elected to the All-Star team, I could really have used the rest to get over my injuries faster.

Willie Randolph was hurting, too, and he was finally replaced on the team, although he went with us to the game so he could get a taste of the All-Star festivities in his rookie year.

American League President Lee MacPhail, who was trying anything to break us out of our All-Star slump, ordered that none of the All-Star pitchers for the American League were supposed to pitch on the Sunday before the game. When Steinbrenner heard this, he was furious and threatened to pitch Hunter on Sunday anyway. MacPhail finally had to go as far as to threaten a possible forfeit, and George backed off. Nothing ever went smoothly.

The All-Star Game was interesting because we played in Philadelphia as part of the nation's Bicentennial celebration, and President Ford was in attendance. He came into the clubhouse before the game, and we stood by our lockers as he walked around shaking hands. I'd never met a President before, so I got a kick out of seeing him in person. I heard later that he told someone I wasn't as big as he thought I was.

For the first-pitch ceremony, the President threw to me and Johnny Bench as the starting catchers, and I've got a nice photograph of the occasion. As for the game, the final score was 7–1, and I don't have to tell you who had the one.

There's no way the National League is so much better than the American League that they should win every single year. I think that's proven in the World Series, which

are divided rather evenly—perhaps the American League
even has an edge. I don't have any good excuses for why the
American League has to embarrass itself every year in the
All-Star Game, but I know it's not because we're twelve or
thirteen times inferior, which has been the margin of de-
feat in recent years.

With the passing of the All-Star break, we were twenty
games over .500 and held a ten-and-a-half-game lead in our
division. People were talking about a runaway, and that
would be okay with us. Pressure games late in the season
are exciting, but, all things considered, I'll take a runaway
any time.

THE PENNANT RETURNS
TO THE BRONX

You have to say this for Billy Martin—he doesn't miss anything. From the first pitch to the final out, he is totally involved in the game, concentrating as intensely as any man in any occupation.

Take the day we played Kansas City and they had to send Hal McRae out to play left field in the ninth inning because someone had been injured. The rule book allows a substitute in such cases to take a few warm-up throws. Billy noticed that McRae took two more than permitted. He protested the game.

Steinbrenner stood behind Billy all the way, going as far as to issue a release saying that if Lee MacPhail didn't uphold the protest, he was failing to do his job. MacPhail denied the protest anyway, and we lost.

The Yankee Stadium scoreboard was another source of controversy in the first year of the new park. For some reason, they built the large playback screen right in the batter's line of vision. As a result, the board couldn't be used when a man was at bat. So immediately the board was half useless, not to mention that the quality of the replays was very weak.

From time to time, the board would follow up close calls with blurry replays. Naturally, the fans saw what they wanted to see, and if the calls were against the Yankees, they hooted and shouted their disapproval of the umpires' call. It only tended to embarrass the umpires and cause them to develop strong anti-Yankee sentiment.

I personally think the quality of umpiring in the American League is getting better. Players are always impressed with an umpire's hustle and desire to be in the right place, and the new young umps who have come into the league in the last few years have done good jobs. Naturally, they blow calls from time to time, and as a catcher, I'll always get my two cents in if I think I'm right. But on the whole, the league can be proud of the caliber of umpiring that has been developing.

Even the organist came in for criticism at the new Stadium. George Steinbrenner likes a lot of music at the ballpark. He plays loud rock music all during batting practice, so you feel you're at a disco rather than a baseball park. And during the game, he likes the organist to pump up enthusiasm, even between pitches.

We had a rookie named Juan Bernhardt with us in 1976—he went on to play for Seattle the following year. Juan came up for his first major league at bat in a key situation, and as the two-strike pitch was on its way, the Stadium suddenly resounded with a loud "dada-da-da-da-da!" Juan was startled by the music, and swung wildly for strike three. Billy didn't know where to direct his anger. He stared at the press box, looking for the organist, looking for anyone, and then, in exasperation, found George. He gave him a disgusted wave of his hand.

Billy always knows where George is sitting, and he can always see George whipping his arm through the air in an-

ger at some piece of strategy. Sometimes, Billy gestures
right back, and it becomes almost a game in itself—except
both men are playing for keeps. George can get excited during a ball game. To him every game is like Ohio State
against Michigan. Once, he got angry and started criticiz-
ing Billy's strategy during a game in which Billy's wife was
sitting with George. Billy was very upset about that one.

Doyle Alexander had become quite a pitcher for us, and
on several occasions flirted with no-hitters. I've never
caught a no-hitter, and we've never been no-hit, for that
matter. In fact, the Yankees haven't been involved in a no-
hitter since 1958, when Hoyt Wilhelm beat them. Wilhelm
pitched for so long that even I faced him late in his career.

I really admire the guys who can play for fifteen or
twenty years. I'd like to be able to do it, but, of course, in
these days, with the salaries so much higher, if a man has
taken care of his money well, there's no need for him to
"hang on." I know I wouldn't want to be in a position to play
after my skills are gone just because I needed the money.

When I think back on my first year with the Yankees,
1969, I recall some of the pitchers in the league, men who
were really throwbacks to a previous era. Names like Dick
Hall, Don McMahon, Juan Pizzaro, Camilo Pascual, Lindy
McDaniel, Al Worthington, Ron Perranoski, Moe Dra-
bowsky, Jim Perry, George Brunet, and, of course, Wilhelm. Maury Wills was still playing in the National
League, and now I play against his son Bump of Texas. I
suppose someday young players will talk of "breaking in
when Munson was still around." I look at Willie Randolph
sometimes and think he might still be playing in 1996, and
it's enough to boggle the mind. I wouldn't be surprised if he
played long enough to see major league baseball expand to
Japan. He might even take regular road trips to Tokyo two
or three times a year.

As the 1976 season moved on, so did the Yankees. We
never faltered as we moved toward the two million mark in

home attendance. We had a four-game losing streak in August, and dropped three in a row to the Angels a few weeks later, but by the end of the month we still had our eleven-and-a-half-game lead, and we seemed out of reach.

We did have a rough trip to Boston in the middle of the summer, our first trip there since the big fight in New York. Mickey Rivers in particular was a target of the Fenway fans, and he wasn't very happy about going out to center field, where he had to listen to some pretty threatening language. He wore his helmet in the outfield for the entire series.

The Commissioner's office even provided us with a security agent to ride the bus with us in Boston. It was like a tale from the early days of baseball, when teams had to slip in and out of town in the dark of night to escape the fans. We won all three of those games in Boston, too, which didn't make the fans any happier.

The season for me was nothing short of super. I started fast and stayed hot all year, never falling under .300. Fifty-four times I had two or more hits in a game. I had seventeen game-winning hits. I was catching real well, and despite the shake-up of our pitching staff in midseason, I was handling the staff well. My confidence was never higher. I felt as though I could set up any hitter in the league after seeing him one time.

Billy had the team running the bases like never before. I stole fourteen, which was only two short of the most steals any catcher made in several decades. Even Nettles stole eleven, after having stolen only two in his previous three seasons.

Actually, we ran a lot more in the first half of the season. Then Randolph had to favor his knee, and we were scoring runs so easily we didn't have to be quite so reckless on the bases. Rivers wound up with forty-three, but when he started the year, we had expected he would break the Yankee record of seventy-four.

My old buddy Gene Michael returned to the Yankees in midseason when Steinbrenner hired him as a coach. He had left under the cloud of a bitter dispute with Gabe Paul, and I'm sure his return caused some battles in the front office. A year later, Stick became part of the front office himself, and then returned to coach first base in 1978. You can just never predict anything about this game.

If the Orioles or the Red Sox or anyone else was going to catch us, time was running out as we headed for September. We opened the month in Baltimore and split four games to remain ten and a half ahead. Then we took two from the Red Sox at home, and the proof of their being hopelessly out of the race was that only 48,000 people showed up for the two games combined.

Although our lead was too much to overcome by the third week of the month, the Orioles came to New York and took four in a row from us. We scored only three runs in the last three games. That brought the lead down to seven and a half with ten to play.

The Tigers hosted us on the 24th for a doubleheader, and after losing our sixth straight in the opener, Grant Jackson got a rare start and beat them 8–0 in the nightcap. The next day, we beat the Tigers 10–6 to clinch the division.

It was our first official champagne party. We couldn't count the one to celebrate being second place in 1970, because only Roy White and I could remember it. We didn't pop the corks until the Orioles lost that evening, as we waited to hear the result of their game by telephone in a Detroit restaurant. When the final out was recorded, we really let loose. Even George and Gabe got a good champagne dousing.

It must have been a very special feeling for Gabe Paul. He'd been in baseball for half a century, and his only taste of triumph had been as traveling secretary with the Cincinnati Reds in 1939 and 1940. He had run a lot of losers since then.

The Yankees rewarded Billy Martin with a new three-year contract, and that was certainly a relief to him. This was the third team he'd led to a division title, but he had yet to win a pennant. Unfortunately, the contract he signed was not a very good one for him. It made him a well-paid manager, as managers go, but there were clauses granting the Yankees the right to fire him without paying him off if he violated club policy regarding such things as the attending of meetings, and the returning of phone calls. When we found this out the following year, we were all surprised that Billy had agreed to such a deal.

We spent the final days of the season just going through the motions, preparing for Kansas City and the playoffs, which the league prefers to call the Championship Series.

I wound up the year with 105 runs batted in, just four behind Lee May, who led the league. I hit .302, had seventeen homers, and played in 152 games, which is just as important to me as any other category. For anyone who wonders whether a multiyear contract detracts from a player's performance, I can cite myself as an example of someone who would never go out in the field to embarrass myself. And in 1976, I certainly didn't embarrass myself at all.

BATTLE TO THE FINISH

I'm not sure I know how bad feelings develop between two clubs. There's not always a fight. We hadn't come close to fighting with the Kansas City Royals, yet there was no love lost as we prepared to face each other in the playoffs.

Billy Martin was having a verbal feud through the newspapers with Larry Gura, the former Yankee pitcher. They had not gotten along well when Gura was in New York. Larry was with the Royals now, and burning to beat us. That put a little fuel on the fire, but honestly, none of us had any hassle with Gura.

Lou Piniella, formerly a Royal, was still very popular with his old teammates and fans. So was Fran Healy, who had joined us in the Gura trade. Still, there was a lot of money on the line, and perhaps that's reason enough to want to beat the other guys so badly.

When the playoff system began in 1969, a lot of critics thought it would produce unworthy World Series competitors—teams without the best records. Many felt the games would be burdensome to the players, and the fans would

150

yawn and wait for the Series. As it turned out, some of the Championship Series have been tremendous, with a lot of memorable moments as well as individual stars.

The reason for their popularity is the intensity with which the teams approach the games. It is well recognized that if a team leads its division after 162 games, it all means pretty little unless the players can win three more and get into the World Series.

Who remembers the 1969 Braves? Does anyone remember that Minnesota won the division in 1969 and 1970? Who did Oakland beat in the 1972 Championship Series? Name the members of the San Francisco Giants' pitching staff from the 1972 National League Championship Series!

The fact is, there is no pennant for the playoff loser. No rings, no place in history, no big check in the mail. You've got to start all over again next year and try to win those three extra games.

So the pattern of the playoffs has gotten a lot more interesting. The players give it their all, and then enjoy just being in the World Series. If they win the World Series, they couldn't be happier. If they lose it, well, they've got nothing to be ashamed of. Where it all counts is in the playoffs.

We flew to Kansas City several days before the series was to open to work out on the artificial surface. It is a whole different game on the synthetic turf, and it does require getting used to. This is one of the few things in baseball that could really be called a home team advantage.

The first game was on Saturday afternoon, October 9, and sure enough, Whitey Herzog selected Gura to work the opener. Larry is a control pitcher. If he's razor sharp, he's tough. But like most control pitchers, who can't rely on the fast ball to blow you down in a pinch, if he's even a drop off with his control, he's in trouble.

Catfish Hunter would pitch for us. The Cat had not had a good year. He was only two games over .500, and for the

first time in six years he'd failed to win twenty games. But
he is one of those players who transcend statistics. If the
money is on the line, you hand him the ball.

Hunter was everything he'd ever been—super. His control was on, his ball was moving, and he limited the Royals
to just five hits. George Brett, who'd popped off in the papers a little, made two errors in the first inning. We scored
two runs and were in command all the rest of the way. Gura
gave up twelve hits, and we beat him 4–1. What was even
more costly for the Royals was the loss of Amos Otis, who
hurt himself running to first in the very first inning. He
was out for the series.

I went one for five in the first game but felt very comfortable and at ease in my first championship game. Perhaps
the tension would build back home in New York, so I was
glad we were opening on the road.

Despite the loss of Otis, the Royals came right back on
Sunday to beat us 7–3. Ed Figueroa, who was only one win
away from becoming the first Puerto Rican to win twenty
games in the majors, failed again, although, of course, it
wouldn't have counted on his regular season statistics. I
had two hits, but I made two errors, so I wasn't feeling too
good after the game. Still, as we flew back to New York, we
knew the advantage was with us, as we had to win only two
of three in our own park. Of course, we couldn't take anything for granted. We had been a better road team in 1976
than a home team, for some reason. We'd won fifty-two on
the road and forty-five at home, which was very unusual for
any team.

Dock Ellis pitched against Andy Hassler in the third
game, and did the job for us. Dock, who would be named the
Comeback Player of the Year in the American League, had
won seventeen during the regular season, and here he was
stopping the Royals 5–3 with a save from Sparky in the
ninth. Chambliss had a homer and drove in three, and I had

two more hits. The two of us were really in good hitting grooves.

Hunter went to the mound in the fourth game to try and wrap it up for us. Needing only one more win, we really wanted to get it over with in game four, if only to get a little rest before the World Series. But everytime I'd start to think of the World Series, I'd quickly remind myself that we still needed twenty-seven more outs before we were there.

Gura started for the Royals again, and neither pitcher was very effective. Gura got knocked out in the third, Hunter in the fourth, and after four innings, the Royals had a 5–2 lead. We really had to admire the way they were playing without Otis in the lineup.

Doug Bird and Steve Mingori each gave up a run in relief, and Graig hit two homers for us, but we fell short, losing 7–4, to even the series. I had two more hits, to give me seven in the four games. Chambliss now had eight.

Well, no matter how you looked at it, the whole season came down to one game. Anyone could win one game—and believe me, there was nothing calm about waiting for sundown and the ball game to begin. I drove to the park thinking of what Dennis Leonard had thrown me in game two, very concerned about the possibility of losing. I take a back seat to no one in terms of optimism (except maybe Houk) and confidence (except maybe Ali), but I'm also a realist. By the time I got to the stadium, I was more determined than ever—we just had to win this one.

The Royals scored twice in the first inning against Figueroa, who hadn't won since September 17. But before we could get down on ourselves, we knocked Leonard out of the game after Rivers, White, and myself all got on, and we wound up tying the game 2–2.

Kansas City came right back in the second with another run, but we reached Splittorff for two in the third to take a

4–3 lead. In the sixth, we scored twice against Andy Hassler to run it up to 6–3, and we began to see the end of this hard-fought series. Figueroa was pitching a gallant game, and we were now nine outs away.

Figgy set the Royals down in the seventh, but in the eighth, after two men got on, Billy came to the mound. We talked it over and decided to bring in Grant Jackson to face Brett. Figueroa got a tremendous ovation as he came off the mound. It was as though the fans had decided the pennant was won, and Ed was the man of the hour.

The fans had been loud all game, but after a while, it just became a constant hum to me. I couldn't hear any distinct voices. It was just like a jet flying over Shea Stadium for three hours.

I concentrated on Grant Jackson as he arrived at the mound. The tying run waited at the plate in the person of George Brett, their best hitter. With one swing of the bat, the roar of the Yankee fans became an unbelievable silence. Brett had cleared the right field fence, and the game was tied. It was as dramatic a home run as we'd seen all year.

Well, it was as though the season was beginning all over again here in the eighth inning of the fifth playoff game. The score was tied 6–6, and it was anybody's game.

Mark Littell got us out in the eighth, and Dick Tidrow got the Royals out in the ninth. Now it was the last of the ninth inning, and Chris Chambliss was first to bat for us. He'd already had one helluva series. He and I each had ten hits for new Championship Series records, and he had also broken a record by driving in seven runs.

I was on the top step of the dugout, fully dressed in my catcher's gear, having made the last out the inning before. Sandy Alomar was in the on-deck circle, since he had run for Carlos May earlier. Nettles, third man up in the inning, was behind me at the bat rack.

It was well past 11 P.M. as Littell took his sign and deliv-

ered to Chris. With that big stocky back of his flashing the
number 10 toward me, Chambliss put all his power into a
pitch and sent it high in the air. As I recall it now, it seemed
as though it was in the air for minutes. Of course, it was all
a matter of a second or two. It cleared the fence, and we all
knew instantly what it meant. The Yankees were American League champions for 1976.

I leaped from the dugout in wild jubilation. In the photos
the next day, I looked as if I were two feet off the ground.
Before Chambliss even reached second, a swarm of fans de-
scended on the field. By the time he was at third, all hope of
reaching the plate was gone. He never did make it. All we
could do was head for the clubhouse and hope Chris made
it. It was a good thing Chris hit the homer instead of a little
guy like Rivers, because Mickey might never have made it
back to the clubhouse.

We were like Little Leaguers in the clubhouse. We had
no idea what was going on outside, but we could be sure the
place was in a state of destruction. Inside, bright television
lights glared, strange faces appeared everywhere, and we
looked for every teammate we could find to embrace with
big bear hugs. Somehow Cary Grant appeared before me—
Steinbrenner had brought him down. I could swear there
were fans in the clubhouse, but I really didn't care. I wasn't
in charge of security. I was in charge of enjoying one of the
happiest moments of my life.

Sure, I was still a young man—twenty-nine years old and
a veteran of only seven big league seasons. But I'd wanted
to play baseball for as long as I could remember, and when
you want to be a baseball player, this is what it's all about.
Winning the pennant!

We were less than forty-eight hours away from the World
Series, but we weren't going to be denied our pennant
party—we celebrated all through the night. I wanted to
make it a night I'd never forget.

Chris Chambliss, who had hit one of the most famous

home runs in the history of baseball, was our "main man" that night, but we each felt the sense of contribution that comes with playing 166 games. Chris hit .524 in the playoffs, and I hit .435. We had earned our celebration, and were making the most of it. Tomorrow would take care of itself.

Here comes Carlton Fisk, headed for home in 1972. Much has been made of our "rivalry" since he came into the league, but a lot of it has been overplayed by the media.

Ralph Houk taught me that I could win more games catching than I could hitting. I always respected him as a manager, and I'll always remember how he stuck by me when I slumped as a rookie.

I always take batting practice seriously. Turning the wrists is the most important part of hitting to me, and I work on it in the cage before every game.

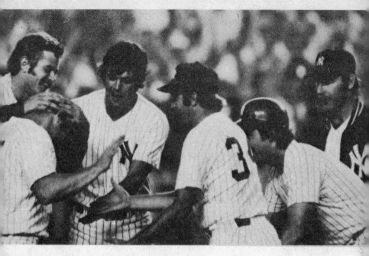

We found ourselves in a pennant race in 1974, and we loved every minute of it until we ran out of time. I won this game with a home run, and here are Rick Dempsey, Lou Piniella, Dick Howser, Bobby Murcer, and Sparky Lyle to meet me at home.

My pal Bobby Bonds and I each received Golden Glove awards in this 1975 photo. As startling as it was to trade Murcer for Bonds, it was just as amazing to see Bonds traded a year later.

A Family Day portrait in 1974. Diana's holding Tracy, and I've got Kelly.

Our first son, Mike, was born in 1975. Do you notice the resemblance to my own baby picture?

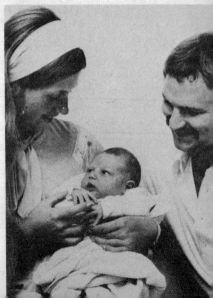

Catfish Hunter (29) joined the Yankees in 1975, and baseball salaries would never be the same again. Here, we're either discussing deferred payments or how to pitch to Rod Carew.

People say I grow beards to make trouble. The truth is, I like beards.
Can there be a more logical reason for growing one?

Above: The moment that Chris Chambliss' pennant-winning home run dropped into the seats was one of the most emotional moments of my career. I leaped from the dugout as Chris raised his arms and Sandy Almar jumped for joy. It was our final victory of 1976. *Right:* Winning the 1976 Most Valuable Player Award capped a great all-around season for me, although we were stopped cold in the World Series. Here I receive the plaque from sportswriter Phil Pepe.

After working on my business interests all day, I love to get to the park and exert physical energy playing ball. Once the game starts, my mind is on nothing but the situation at hand.

A controversial play at home involving Steve Garvey and myself in the 1977 World Series. The question was whether I had tagged Steve before he reached the plate. I just turned and tagged and had no idea of whether I got him or not.

Joe DiMaggio threw out the first ball in the final game of the 1977 World Series. In my mind, I was thinking that this might be my final game as a Yankee.

By the time we had won the 1977 pennant, I was drained both physically and emotionally. It was hard to feel like celebrating after so much of the fun had gone out of the game for me.

Not talking to the press didn't enhance my public image in 1978, but it made me a happier person, as I was able to avoid the daily barrage of questions over upsetting subjects. All in all, I was in a good frame of mind as 1978 dawned.

THE TALENTED
MR. BENCH

I guess we didn't leave the stadium until well after two in the morning. The stadium lights were still bright and there were a lot of people milling around outside. I tried not to think about the fact that in eight hours, we'd be back at the park, boarding a bus for Cincinnati.

Sure enough, there we were, still glowing from the events of the night before, ready to take our first trip as American League champions. We had two buses, because our wives were all coming. There was such chaotic joy in the air that Billy Martin invited a bunch of batboys, some excess batting practice pitchers, and a handful of stadium cops aboard. They all came with us to Cincinnati—no luggage and no phone calls home.

We'd land in Cincinnati in a couple of hours, go to the park for a workout, and then to our hotel, which was about a half hour out of the city.

Aside from the fact that they are a very talented team, the Reds were well rested. Everyone seemed to be picking them for those two reasons. As for me, I was determined to have some fun and never forget that I'd been here. Who knew if I'd ever be in another World Series?

Diana and I were both amazed at how baseball-crazy Cincinnati seemed to be. New York fans are enthusiastic, but New York is so big you can easily find a place where people have never even heard of baseball. In Cincinnati, it seemed as though the whole city was painted Red. I must have seen 500 kids on the streets with Pete Rose T-shirts, his big red number 14 on the back.

Riverfront Stadium seemed massive—all enclosed, with thousands of outfield seats on many levels. There are no parks like that in the American League. I decided it's not a bad park, and the visitors' clubhouse is nice.

The field is artificial, which we were pretty well used to by now, and our workout was smooth and professional, but we were all still "up" from the night before. I knew we'd have to get over the euphoria and get our minds on the Reds in a hurry.

The trip to the park for the first game the next day was funny. It started out with everyone grumbling about their series tickets—where were they, who had them, how come they were so lousy, etc. Finally, Dock Ellis stood up and began reading passages from his newly published book, trying to get us psyched up for Cincinnati. He read to us the portions about his brushing back the Reds' hitters, and we couldn't stop laughing.

The bus had a lot of trouble making a tight turn into the tunnel below the stadium, and we hit the wall. That caused more laughter on the bus; then, as far as I was concerned, we were ready to play ball.

But once you step on the field for a World Series game, you know immediately that this is a big event. There are 250 reporters standing around the batting cage, interviewing one another, being seen, and occasionally saying something like "How ya' doin', Thurman?"

The field is cleared long before the game starts, and all

you see are officials from the commissioner's office preparing for things like the first ball ceremony, the National Anthem, the player's introductions, the bands, and all the glitter.

It was bitter cold that first day—October 16—and we had portable heaters brought into the dugouts.

When fans see the players come out of the dugout during the introductions, they don't even realize that we can't hear a thing. The public-address systems aren't designed to be heard in the dugouts, and we know to run out only when a league official says "Go!" And since it's so unusual to open a baseball game that way, I always feel as if I'm with the Boston Celtics or something when I run out there.

Billy surprised a lot of people, including our starting pitcher, when he named Doyle Alexander to open the series. Doyle hadn't appeared in the playoffs and was well rested, and Billy was just taking a gamble that he'd baffle the Reds, as he had handcuffed many American League teams all summer.

The Reds opened with Don Gullett. Ironically, both starting pitchers would in a few weeks become free agents. Both were pitching their last games for their respective teams and would soon be highly sought after.

Elliott Maddox was in right field for us, which was also something of a surprise, since it was no secret that he and Billy didn't get along very well. Their feud carried over from Detroit and Texas.

Gullett got off to a fast start. He struck out Rivers, got White to ground out, and I went down swinging. In the last of the first, with two out, Joe Morgan homered to right. We were down 1–0.

I was enjoying talking with the Cincinnati players as they came to bat. I'd met some of them at All-Star Games or at golf tournaments, and I was being very chatty and friendly. Several of them later remarked that I seemed to be the only guy on the Yankees enjoying myself.

I was glad to be playing against Bench, whom I admire a great deal, and it was good to see guys like Rose, Morgan, and Perez, whom I'd known before. They sure were a great team, at least offensively, and believe me, we never sold them short.

We scored in the second on a sacrifice fly by Nettles, who had led the American League in home runs. But a sacrifice fly by Rose put the Reds on top 2–1 after three.

Gullett continued to hold us in check, and the Reds were able to add a run in the sixth and two in the seventh. We had a chance to score in the sixth when White reached on an error and I got my first Series hit, a single to right. When Piniella followed with a looping liner over second, Morgan ran it down, and our threat ended.

We got Gullett out of the game in the eighth when he injured his ankle pitching to Rivers. Pedro Borbon came in, but we couldn't solve him, either, and we lost the first game 5–1.

The second game was to be played on Sunday night. It was really strange hanging around the hotel all day Sunday, so I was glad Diana was with me, and we spent our time talking with the other guys and their wives.

It was really cold at the ball park that night, but, down 1-0, we had to forget things like the weather and concentrate on winning. Catfish was to go for us, and Fred Norman, an old American Leaguer, for them. We turned to Cat when we needed the win, and he was there to do the job. It proved to be a pivotal game in the series—if we could win, we'd go home even, which was fine. If not, we'd be in fast trouble.

Catfish had trouble in the second, allowing three runs and four hits, but we came pecking back, and he got stronger. In the fourth, I beat out a hit to Rose at third, and Nettles brought me in later with a single. It was 3–1.

In the seventh, we scraped together two more to tie the game, with my ground ball bringing in the tying run. So here we were, in another ninth-inning situation, and we'd really played a good game.

Dave Concepcion opened the Reds' ninth by flying out. Rose flied to Roy in left. Two outs, no one on, Ken Griffey the batter. He hit a slow grounder to Fred Stanley at shortstop, and "Chicken" scooped it up but threw it into the Reds' dugout for a two-base error. We intentionally walked Morgan to face Perez, but Tony lined a single to left and it was over. We lost, 4–3.

Back in New Jersey, my phone didn't stop ringing. Everyone wanted tickets to the World Series, the first to be played in Yankee Stadium in twelve years. I couldn't believe how many people had gotten my telephone number.

Billy Martin was a nervous wreck at this point. He had endured a great deal during the season, and was feeling a lot of pressure now as we had our backs to the wall. Teams had come back from 2–0 deficits before, but Billy wasn't exactly Mr. Optimism. He could get testy with writers, and now he was in no mood to seek any confrontations.

Each day during a World Series, a press conference is held at the downtown hotel headquarters. Both managers are expected to attend, but no one could interest Billy in it. Finally, I was asked to represent the Yankees, as team captain. I wasn't crazy about going downtown on the day of the series, but I did it, and I fielded all the questions. Yes, we know we're down 2–0. No, we haven't given up. Yes, I think we can still win. No, the Reds aren't that much better than us. Yes, we were tired after the playoffs. No, I'm not making alibis.

Dock Ellis was our man in game three, and Pat Zachry was the Reds' pitcher. Man, it was cold. Only the commissioner sat there without four sweaters and a topcoat. It was his decision to play at night, for the benefit of television, and he wasn't going to look cold for anyone.

The third game was very depressing. The Reds scored three times off Dock in the second inning, and finally knocked him out in the fourth. We were down 4–0 before we got on the scoreboard. We made it 4–2 in the seventh when Jim Mason, of all people, hit a home run. But the Reds came right back to score two in the eighth, and that would be all the scoring. We lost 6–2, and were down 3–0. No team had ever come back from that margin to win.

Our clubhouse was very somber. There was no shame in losing, but we did want to win at least one game in the series.

In the fourth game, also at night, I scored a run in the first inning to put us in the lead for the first time in the series. But Johnny Bench homered in the fourth off Figueroa, and the Reds had a 3–1 lead. Bench hit one into the left field seats, a place few men had reached during the regular season. We got one back in the fifth to trail 3–2, and we hung close behind Figgy's pitching. But in the ninth, Cincinnati scored four times, with Bench hitting another homer to clinch his MVP award for the series. It was also a shot to left field. In the entire season, only seventeen balls had been hit there by right-hand hitters, and Bench had just put two there in one game. The guy is really something!

Billy was ejected when he threw a baseball across the field in disgust. I could feel his frustration—it had not been an easy season. By the bottom of the ninth, we were a beaten team. We were retired in order, and the Reds had swept us in four straight games.

Hidden in the gloom was the fact that I'd gone four for four in the final game, tying a record for most hits in a game, and bringing my series average up to .529, highest ever for a player on a losing team. I had six straight hits going back to game three for another series record. From a personal standpoint, I had nothing to be ashamed of.

Next to the Yankee clubhouse was the postgame interview room. Bob Fishel of the American League office asked me to come in and represent the Yankees again, and I did. I walked in and got on the stage as Sparky Anderson, the Reds manager, was speaking.

"Munson is an outstanding ballplayer and he would hit .300 in the National League," he was saying, "but don't ever compare anybody to Johnny Bench, don't never embarrass nobody by comparing them to Johnny Bench. "

I couldn't believe what I was hearing—I don't know if he was aware I was standing there. I'd read a lot about the class Anderson was supposed to have. This is how he behaved after winning a world championship? I didn't want to get into a hassle with him, but I was really mad about what I'd just heard. I went to the microphone and said, "For me to be belittled after the season I had and after the game I had . . . it's bad enough to lose, but worse to be belittled like that."

"To win four in a row and rub it in my face, that's class," I said with sarcasm. "I never compared myself to Johnny Bench, but if I played in the National League, I might be the best offensive player in the league."

By now Bench had come into the room. "Nice going, J.B.," I said to him. "Super." And he was.

I had played a terrific World Series, but the embarrassment of being swept took a lot out of it. Also, the Anderson remarks had left a bitter taste with me, and I wish I could shut off my memory at the end of the playoffs. I had played the games and had some fun, and then Anderson had to display such poor taste.

A few days later, he told the newspapers he had sent me a letter of apology. All I know is that to this day I've never received it. I guess he just felt he could restore some of his lost class by telling the reporters he'd sent one.

The season was over and it was October 21, about a month later than we usually ended our seasons. There would follow a fast but eventful winter.

MOST VALUABLE PLAYER

I was very interested in the Most Valuable Player voting. All through the World Series, people had spoken of my being a cinch for the award, and I'd have to admit that I would have been let down if the award hadn't come to me. Of course, I was well aware the award was bestowed by the baseball writers, and I never had established a great relationship with them.

From time to time, I've sworn off talking to the writers. If I say something good, they'll probably not use it; and if I say something bad, it will get blown out of proportion. I've seen too many guys get so hung up with the press that it's worked against them personally and professionally.

My feeling is that athletes are paid to play ball, and we were given these talents much as pianists, painters, carpenters, and mechanics are given theirs. But somewhere along the line, it was determined that an athlete had to have the ability to talk. He has to be glib on TV and radio and wordy for sportswriters. I don't know how that developed, but the result is that now players get branded as "good guys" or "troublemakers" just based on how they react to the press.

Alex Johnson never had a good word for the press, so he was described as a "bad guy." Where did it ever say that the press was the final judge of a man's character? Suppose Alex was great to his family and friends, and treated children especially nice? As long as he didn't care to discuss matters with the writers, he was a "bad guy."

When Alex was with the Angels, he had a disagreement with Chico Ruiz, and Chico pulled a gun on him. Fortunately, he didn't use it. A couple of years later, Chico was killed in an auto accident. In the meantime, Alex's reputation had been withered to bits by the press. It's amazing how many people remember Alex as having "shot and killed Chico Ruiz." It's just an example of how the press can influence readers to believe anything they want about a man.

Well be that as it may, twenty-four writers were now to decide who the American League's MVP would be. I wasn't going to pretend to be uninterested, and I called the Yankee office several times to see if there was any news. The announcement was to be made at 6 P.M. so it could make the morning papers.

Finally, at 3 P.M., my phone rang. It was the Yankee office to say I'd won, and I'd won big. Eighteen of the twenty-four writers had selected me for first place. I had four seconds and two thirds, and won by eighty-seven points over George Brett. Mickey Rivers was third, Hal McRae fourth, and Chris Chambliss fifth, so the Yankees were well represented.

Diana and I headed downtown for a hastily called press conference, which was not very well attended, no doubt because of the unusual hour. It was too late for television to tape, and the afternoon papers had already been published.

"I'm proud that I won," I told those present. "I know it wasn't politics. I won this on my ability."

The press made a lot of my being named captain and winning the award in the same year. George and Gabe were in the room. I know it must have been a good moment for George, who had named me captain, but I made a remark about a "new contract," which seemed to catch him by surprise.

The photographers called Diana up to the podium, and we posed for some photos—and that's what happens when you win the MVP award. You don't get any bonus for it, but you get a nice plaque the following year—and let's make no mistake about it, I was damn proud of it.

Along with my All-American honor in 1968, the MVP award was the best thing that had ever happened to me in sports. If people thought I was cocky before, for the next few days, I'd really be holding my head up high.

Not long before the MVP announcement came the re-entry draft for free agents. Bill Campbell was the first to sign from it, and got a few million dollars from the Red Sox. The free agent system, which George had predicted would never come about, had happened, and I could see what kind of money I would have been in a position to make had I not signed a multiyear pact the previous spring. Still, George had made good on his word in keeping me the highest-salaried player, so I expected him to redo the contract now that we had won the pennant.

True to form, as in their aggressive pursuit of Hunter, Messersmith, and Blue, the Yankees were out and battling for the free agents. Only two would be permitted, and Don Gullett was the first one signed. They had a big press conference for him, and the Yankee office asked me to attend, as captain, and formally "welcome" Don to New York. I went, even though I was wearing a hunting vest and looked like a slob.

The Yankees were next interested in Bobby Grich, but when they were convinced he was going to play in California, they switched direction to go after Reggie Jackson before he got away.

I guess Reggie is George's kind of guy. The gift of gab, the New York flashiness, the confident air, all made him a superstar to George. And he made Reggie the highest-paid of all the free agents, the biggest star out of the draft.

Naturally, the press conference for Reggie was a mob scene, with him calling all the writers by their first names, and asking the names and affiliations of those he didn't know before responding. What a beauty. I was there because the office had asked me to be present for this one, too.

Well, it was time to talk to George about a new contract. When I brought up the fact that we'd won the pennant, he said he had told me he'd rewrite the contract if we won the *World Series*. Obviously, one of us had heard the wrong thing—I didn't think it was me.

Now came the question of salary.

Players are now allowed to call the Players' Association and ask what other players earn. It's a way of determining your value. So I called Marvin Miller's office to find out what Gullett and Jackson were making. They got back to me and said, "Funny thing, those are the only two contracts that haven't been filed in the league office."

Well, I signed another contract, but I told the Yankee lawyer who was present that this wasn't to be the last contract, and he'd better think about preparing yet another.

At a banquet in Syracuse, I talked about my current hassle, saying I wanted to be traded if George wasn't going to keep his word. No one picked it up as a news story, and I don't think it ever got back to New York. I'd have heard about it, because George hates to read anything bad about himself in the papers. It's one way to really get to him and to get results.

A few days later, at a speaking engagement I had in Canada, the wire services picked up my comments. It was all over the papers in New York. George called me at home at 1:00 A.M. in the midst of a card game with some friends. He said he wanted me to come to New York right away to sign a press release saying the story was wrong. I knew I'd gotten to him.

I flew to New York the next day, and by now, I knew exactly what Reggie Jackson would be earning as salary. When the session in George's office was over, I had gotten a lot of money up front. Some other financial considerations of immediate importance to me were taken care of, too. But at the key moment, with my pen poised over a new contract, I looked at George and said, "Am I the highest-salaried player on this club?"

He told me I was, but I knew better. I don't want to go into specific figures here for several reasons. First of all, it's not my place to say what Jackson or Gullett made. Secondly, I'm making a lot of money, so my complaints can really sound petty. Suffice it to say the Yankees have taken good care of my family and me. I owe a great deal, in terms of wealth, to them. I signed that contract because it gave me a lot of money in the first year, which I could put to good use quickly. My only disagreement with George was over what I considered to be a breach of our understanding.

Although baseball salaries are high today, I think they need to be considered in their proper perspective. There are only 650 major league baseball players in the entire country. Each of us has a skill owned by the minutest percentage of people in America. Those at the top of their professions in industry, banking, commerce, insurance, and so many other professions earn salaries even higher. You can pick up business magazines and see what those salaries are for corporate executives.

Not only do we provide entertainment for millions, but for the club owners, we generate millions of dollars in ticket sales, television and radio rights, and parking and concession commissions. And we increase the personal prestige of the owners. People don't turn on the TV or buy a season box to watch George Steinbrenner own a team— they come to see the players play.

The Players' Association points out that teams have met their entire player payroll before opening day, just on their TV and radio money, and the money in the bank on season ticket sales. For a long time, the owners held control of the bulk of that money, and as a businessman, I can appreciate their position. But the game has changed now, the players are getting a bigger cut, and rather than lament that players are overpaid, people should realize that players were long underpaid, and things are finally, after more than 100 years of major league baseball, beginning to straighten out.

So it was an eventful winter which failed to leave me in the best frame of mind. Before I knew it, it was time to head for Fort Lauderdale again, for what would prove to be a nerve-racking and difficult season.

REGGIE "STIRS" THINGS UP

When you come off a World Series, everyone expects you to get into another one. So naturally, all eyes would be on us from the first day of training camp. And with our free agents on the team, it was all the more certain that we would spend the season playing under a magnifying glass. Nothing would escape public attention except perhaps our performance on the field.

Of course, attention was focused on Reggie from the day he arrived in camp. He loves playing in the spotlight, and anyone who could become a big-name star in Oakland obviously has the ability to excite the fans and the media—Reggie was a big name even before the A's became a good team.

Some players like a lot of attention, and some don't. Publicity for a teammate is not scorned, and it seldom causes any form of jealousy. We knew, of course, that Reggie loved the limelight, and this was one of the reasons he wanted to play in New York.

What we didn't fully understand was his need to prove his leadership. In Oakland, Sal Bando had been the team captain, and Reggie had done his job by producing a lot of runs. There had been no indication that he had ever craved Sal's title or had made an effort to take over his leadership role.

In spring training, though, we felt from the start that Reggie was looking at himself as a leader. No one thought he was trying to get the captaincy from me—he just seemed to want to be quickly recognized as the on-field leader of the club.

Well, as far as I was concerned, let Reggie be Reggie. I wasn't so hung up on being captain that he was going to disturb me. My concern was that the man produce his 100 RBIs and avoid any dissension on the club. He could lead as much as he wanted if he could give us what we needed.

Two weeks into spring training writer Robert Ward came to do a story on Reggie for *Sport* Magazine. Reggie was familiar with *Sport* because they had given him a sports car for being the hero of the 1973 World Series, when most people thought Bert Campaneris should have won it. The magazine's editor knew that giving the award to Reggie would be more rewarding to them in terms of publicity.

Reggie really opened up to Ward and even insisted that Ward print certain remarks about me. Reggie knew that if *Sport* was interviewing him, it would probably be for a major story, maybe a cover story. And Ward, who had been sizing up Reggie's mood and gaining his confidence, asked questions to draw him out.

What came out in print some weeks later was Reggie saying ". . . this team . . . it all flows from me. I've got to keep it all going. I'm the straw that stirs the drink. It all comes back to me. Maybe I should say me and Munson . . . but really he doesn't enter into it. He's being so damned insecure about the whole thing. I've overheard him talking about me . . . I'll hear him telling some other writer that he wants it to be known that he's the captain of

the team, that he knows what's best. Stuff like that. And
when anybody knocks me, he laughs real loud so I can
hear . . ."

The article continued, "Munson's tough too. He *is* a winner, but there is just nobody who can do for a club what I
can do. . . . There is nobody who can put meat in the seats
that way I can. That's just the way it is. . . . Munson
thinks he can be the straw that stirs the drink, but he can
only stir it bad.

"It's so apparent, why can't Munson and Chambliss and
all the rest of them understand the sheer simplicity . . .
the cold logic?

"Don't you see, that there is just no way I can play second
fiddle to *anybody*. Hah! That's just not in the cards.
. . . There ain't no way!"

The story didn't come out until the season had already
opened, but *Sport* put out prereleases to generate publicity.

I tend to shrug off a bad story about myself—and I've certainly had my share, since I don't have a love affair with
the media as Reggie does. But to get ripped in a national
magazine with such immature statements . . . well, that
was just a little bit too much. And it's remarkable to think
that Reggie would say such things only *two weeks* into
spring training, when he hardly knew anyone and was just
beginning to get himself settled with a new ball club.

The statements were damaging not because of my feelings, but because they split the team. There was no need to
make an issue out of the leadership question, because it
was never anything I flaunted.

What the article really did was bring out a lot of Reggie's
own insecurities. The thought that I might be jealous of
him is preposterous. I have things in life that Reggie can
only hope to have—a stable family life with a wonderful
wife and three great children; a secure private business life
which has kept my head in the real world and provided life-

time security for my family; genuine friends, maintained from my years in Canton.

Reggie's whole life is based on the unreal world of baseball. He has no stable family, no great business knowledge. His friends are those who tell him how great he is, and if they're celebrities, all the better. He wants badly to be the guy people look up to, but they do for one reason only—he's a baseball star.

The Reggie issue really never went away. Early in the season, when we had gotten off to a poor start, Steinbrenner realized the effect it was having on the club. He told me I better start getting along with Reggie or Billy would be in a lot of trouble.

Imagine that! I was suddenly put in the middle and made responsible for Billy's job. I wish now I hadn't gone along with Steinbrenner, but I got Fran Healy to bring Jackson to me for a talk to try and patch things up.

The wounds didn't exactly heal, but we cleared the air a little. I challenged Reggie to name one thing he had that I would want, just to clear up this jealousy matter. He didn't even answer me.

After that talk, we were able at least to say hello to each other. We even had some conversations. But I think he felt very uncomfortable and self-conscious about our relationship. I think when I confronted him with the reality of life—that baseball may be a great ego trip, but there's a lot more to this world than baseball—he found himself unable to deal with it. For the sake of the team, we did no more interviews on each other. But we didn't become the best of friends, either.

Despite how good we looked on paper, our 1977 season was not off to the fast start people predicted. That's because the pitching staff was quite shaky. A rotation of Catfish Hunter, Don Gullett, Ed Figueroa, Dock Ellis and Ken Holtzman was supposed to get us going. But Hunter, Gullett, and Figueroa all experienced arm trouble, Ellis got into a contract dispute with Steinbrenner, and Holtzman, it was decided, could not help us, and so he was relegated to infrequent appearances from the bullpen.

Two things saved us. First, we were able to trade Dock to Oakland for Mike Torrez. With Dock in a bad frame of mind, it was doubtful he was going to help us. And Torrez, a big and strong right-hander, was off to a fast start with the A's. It was a trade made in the nick of time.

Our other advantage was the emergence of Ron Guidry. The frail-looking lefty from Louisiana had barely made the team in spring training. He was wild and couldn't get anyone out, and finally made the team by default, since the farm system wasn't turning out a lot of competition. Guidry opened the season in the bullpen, but when Billy had to turn to him in desperation, he emerged as our most effective starter. Seldom do you see anyone come out of nowhere as Ron did—and on a team like we had, he was certainly our least likely candidate for stardom.

We had a five-game losing streak and a six-game winning streak all in the first few weeks of the season. We were barely playing .500 ball when Guidry made his first start on April 29 and shut out Seattle 3–0 as I hit a two-run homer. I was hitting well, and felt better physically than I had in years.

We swept the Mariners and I hit a home run in each of the three games as we started to move. On May 2, Bucky Dent hit a grand slam as we beat the Angels 8–1.

Bucky had joined us just before opening day in a trade with the White Sox. We had some mixed feelings about the deal, although not about Bucky himself. Fred Stanley was suddenly out of a regular job after doing such good work the year before at shortstop. Fortunately, he had signed a big multiyear contract before the trade, and so he had great security. And Oscar Gamble, who had been very popular with the players, was sent to Chicago in the eleventh-hour deal. Oscar was actually called off the bus and told of the trade as we were preparing to open the season. That's a tough way to get the news, but it's a price you pay for not signing. Oscar was far apart in his negotiations with the Yankees, and any player in that situation now has to expect to be traded, since the team would otherwise lose him after the season and get nothing in return. At least Oscar had a great year in Chicago and then made a lot of money as a free agent.

By May 7, we were in first place, and the next day I had four hits, including a homer. Everywhere I went, people wanted to know how Reggie and I were getting along. I tried to keep my mind on baseball and off Reggie, but the press didn't let up. Meanwhile, Reggie was not hitting well, and George and Billy were beginning to disagree over where he should hit in the lineup. Billy was hitting him fifth, and George insisted that Jackson belonged in the cleanup spot.

The race stayed close, and we were in and out of the top spot, but Reggie still wasn't hitting much, and his fielding was disappointing. By late June, as we headed for Boston, tempers were beginning to grow short. Reggie was unhappy in New York. He felt the fans and the press were against him, and that Billy Martin wasn't hitting him cleanup because the Yankees never had a black superstar with, according to him, a 160 IQ and didn't know how to deal with one.

Things came to a head in Fenway Park on June 18 before a national television audience. Reggie relaxed on a base hit to right and let the hitter turn it into a double. Without hesitating, Billy sent Paul Blair out to right field to replace Jackson.

Jackson, startled, came into the dugout and went straight for Martin, looking for an explanation. In a flash, the two were ready to go at each other, and only the coaches kept them from coming to blows. Jackson wisely retreated to the clubhouse, and the game continued. But the whole incident had been witnessed by a capacity crowd and a network TV audience—not an everyday sight!

We lost all three games in Boston, and at that point, Steinbrenner began to have serious thoughts about changing managers. Furthermore, he didn't make a secret of it, hinting to writers that he couldn't tolerate seeing his manager lose control in the dugout during a game. George had been in Reggie's corner from the day he signed, and Reggie seemed to have George's sympathy in this incident. Billy was being publicly embarrassed not only by Jackson, but also by Steinbrenner, and the pressures were starting to build on him.

We lost five straight starting with the Boston series, and people were starting to count us out. But when the Red Sox came to New York on June 24, Billy got a hero's reception from the fans as he took the lineup out. It really pumped him up for this important series.

There were 55,000 fans in the park that night, and they were pretty quiet as we trailed 5–3 going to the last of the ninth. Catfish had been tagged for three homers, and it was a depressing scene.

But when Willie Randolph tripled and Roy White hit a dramatic, game-tying home run, the place woke up. It was perhaps the most important hit we had all year because it seemed to wake us up, too.

I couldn't have been happier for Roy—the senior member of our team and a first-rate gentleman. When I once had a testimonial dinner in Canton, Roy was the one man I asked to come. I'm proud to have been a teammate of Roy White's for so many years.

As though the script was written in Hollywood, we won that game 6–5 on an eleventh-inning hit by Reggie. With that big win, we went on to sweep the series with Boston, as the Red Sox proceeded to lose ten straight. Suddenly, we were alive again.

Reggie was a happy man after his gamer. He even shook hands with his teammates. A few days earlier, while in a more brooding mood, he had failed to shake anyone's hand after a home run—he said his hand hurt.

Although we were playing better ball, Billy's situation wasn't improving. Steinbrenner wasn't backing him, and rumors continued to fly. He might have been gone by this time, had Dick Howser said yes when offered the job, but Dick turned it down. It seemed like Billy was on the verge of being fired every other day.

Billy Martin is a man I respect. He has great sensitivity—perhaps too much for his own good. He is a very warm person, but his feelings can be hurt easily. Nobody makes friends more easily than Billy, just as no one gets into battles as quickly as Billy. Sometimes, he can be his own worst enemy just by sticking to his guns. I will always admire the man, though, as a manager and as a person.

In Baltimore in early July, the pressure was really getting to him. He spoke to me about it, and particularly about his concern for his family if he got fired. He had signed that contract which gave the Yankees a lot of ways to avoid paying him off—now it was coming back to haunt him.

As we spoke, tears welled up in his eyes. To avoid having anybody see him so upset, we took a walk around the block until he could clear the air a little. I felt very close to Billy that day.

Our next stop after Baltimore was Milwaukee. George arrived in town—something he seldom does, especially in Milwaukee. At once, rumors were hot, and they weighed heavily not only on Billy, but on all of us.

After a night game, Lou Piniella and I had a couple of drinks at Sally's, a restaurant near the lake. We got to talking about the deteriorating situation on the club, and about how unlikely it looked that we could still win the pennant under such a gloomy cloud. At about half past midnight, our courage up a little, we decided to see Steinbrenner and tell him our feelings.

We knocked on his hotel room door and woke him up. He opened the door in his pajamas, and we went in. Our meeting was agreed to be confidential, with one purpose only—to stabilize the situation so that we could concentrate on playing ball. What we said to Steinbrenner was "You've got to get off Billy's back. You're driving him crazy. If you're going to fire him, then fire him. If you're not, leave him alone and let him manage."

After about two hours, there was a knock on the door. George opened it, and there was Billy. His suite was on the same floor, and he'd heard voices, so he knocked. We felt a little sheepish for a second because we knew it looked conspiratorial to Billy. He brought that up in a hurry, and we told him right out the exact reason we were there.

I was very pleased with what came out of the meeting, for Billy's sake, at least. While George wouldn't commit himself to Billy's future with the Yankees, he did finally agree to guarantee his salary. If nothing else, Billy could relax about his security. He might be fired tomorrow, but he would be paid for three full seasons.

Around the time of our Milwaukee meeting, a story quoted an unnamed player as saying that George was calling the shots from upstairs and dictating the lineup to Billy.

George reacted angrily and decided the player was Carlos May—probably the least likely player to blast anyone in the papers. But George had been annoyed by Carlos' failure to lose weight, and his refusal to sign, so he was a good fall guy.

I went to George to straighten that out. "Carlos wasn't the man," I told him. "I was! I gave out those quotes, and I believe they're accurate. So stop picking on Carlos."

Well, now we got to Kansas City, and George decides to have a clubhouse meeting—a "pep talk" to get us up for the second half of the season. But it didn't work out that way. He lectured us and threatened us, and finally he jumped on anonymous players who leak things to the press.

Here I had gone to the man on my own and told him I had made the statements. My teammates knew I had done that to get Carlos off the hook. And now, right in front of me and all my teammates, he was making me look like a liar—as though no one had confessed to the quotes! I was stunned.

So as the All-Star Game arrived, I was in a bad frame of mind. Jackson's magazine story bugged me, I felt deceived over my contract, and I felt I'd been made to look like a fool in Kansas City. Everything was coming down on me at once.

Fisk outpolled me again, so he started the All-Star Game in Yankee Stadium, but I really couldn't care anymore. By now, I was more determined than ever to get out of New York. The problems at the ball park made me feel closer to Diana and the children, and seek more gratification from my business interests. It all added up to my wanting to go home, where I could play ball in peace and attend to the things in life that matter to me.

I'm not a controversial person. I don't go popping off to the press, I don't look for publicity, and I don't create trouble. I'm the guy Steinbrenner would turn to when he needed an intermediary to settle a dispute with a player. I'm the guy called upon to represent the players at the Gullett and Jackson signings. Now, suddenly, I'm in the middle of this whole mess.

THE YANKEES
PREVAIL AGAIN

After the All-Star Game, George called me. He said he saw things getting out of hand, and he felt there was no way we could still win with Billy. I said, "Hey, what do you want me to say? It's up to you—do what you want."

He asked me about the other players, and I told him the truth—nobody was going to walk out on him if Billy got fired. They're all paid to play, and that's what they'd do.

He continued to brood over the matter, and I'm sure came very close to making the decision. To the press, he continued to say it was all up to Gabe Paul.

A few days later, we postponed a game against Kansas City, even though it stopped raining at about 5 P.M. The Yankees said the grounds were unplayable and more rain was forecast. The Royals were mad because they would have to return to New York in September to play a single game.

George used the occasion to call in a group of writers and discuss Martin with them. Such candor was highly unusual. George listed seven rules by which he would judge Billy's performance as manager:

1. Does he win?
2. Does he work hard enough?
3. Is he emotionally equipped to lead men?
4. Is he organized?
5. Does he understand human nature?
6. Is he prepared for each game?
7. Is he honorable?

To subject Billy to this kind of public scorekeeping—to let every fan in the country sit back and make his own judgment—was pushing things to the brink. I couldn't believe Billy would stand for it. But his love for the Yankees was deep and genuine, and he was determined not to buckle under.

Now controversies multiplied. Every series produced something new. The Brewers series had brought the conversation between George and me. The Royals series had brought forth the press gathering on Billy's future. Now the Orioles came to town, and our supposedly "confidential" meeting in Milwaukee blew open.

Phil Pepe, a reputable New York sportswriter, phoned me to say that Steinbrenner had told him all about the meeting and implied that Piniella and I recommended firing Billy.

I never said a word to Steinbrenner about the matter which we had agreed was confidential. But I told Piniella about it, and he was madder than hell. He called Steinbrenner up and told him off. Ol' Lou will never hesitate to speak his mind, whether he's telling off the boss, chiding his teammates, or getting on Reggie's case.

I hit my 100th career homer against the Orioles on July 28 in a 14–2 victory, and after the game, Steinbrenner had a magnum of champagne sent to the clubhouse for me. I was sure he did it because he knew I was perturbed over the Pepe story. He even called and denied having talked with Phil at all.

What's going on here, I thought to myself. This is just one story after another that isn't checking out.

I was having another good year and, in fact, by the end of July had a decent shot at repeating the MVP award. But I was having more and more trouble coping. August turned out to be a disastrous month for me, although the club did start to take off, in spite of continued strife.

Suddenly everything seemed to be falling apart at once. Holtzman called Steinbrenner a fool for signing him to a big contract and then letting him sit in the bullpen all year. Reggie was unhappy. He hinted that his contract had an escape clause which would allow him to get out of town after the season—a clause which did not in fact exist.

Hunter's arm continued to trouble him, and then it was announced he had a hernia.

Don Gullett and Ed Figueroa were sent to Los Angeles for examination of arm problems. We met with loud protest against our walkie-talkie system between the press box and the dugout. In Chicago, Bill Veeck hired a clown to stand beside Gene Michael for the entire game and ridicule our walkie-talkies.

We lost two straight in Seattle, and Billy, in tears, had to ask the writers to leave.

Piniella yelled at everyone after the Seattle losses, particularly those who were saying they wanted to be traded.

Jackson was charged with assault on a kid in the stadium parking lot after the All-Star Game. He was cleared in a trial later.

Steinbrenner apologized to the people of New York for the way the club was playing. Gabe Paul issued a statement telling us to cut the B.S. and start playing.

Hunter and Torrez criticized Martin on an Oakland radio show for not having a set pitching rotation.

And the beat went on. The guys who were having good years kept us rolling. Dent, Chambliss, Randolph, Nettles, Lyle, and Guidry were all doing fine jobs, although by September, Chambliss and White were tailing off and Billy began to platoon them, moving Cliff Johnson and Dave Kingman in and out of the lineup.

Nettles was doing especially well. After another bad start, he was making a real run at another home run title. His fielding at third was brilliant. Jackson was driving in almost a run a game. On August 20, despite everything, we had moved to within one and a half games of Boston.

I was having a miserable month, though. I think I drove in six runs the entire month of August and must have hit a hundred and change. The rest of the lineup was carrying me.

I grew a beard on the Western trip that month, and it created quite a story. Since Diana hates my beard, the only time I grow one is when I'm on a long road trip. I knew the Yankees wouldn't press the matter, because if I made a grievance out of it, I would surely win. But I didn't grow it for that reason—I just grew it because I like wearing a beard.

Naturally, all the writers were convinced I was growing it to defy Steinbrenner's edict against beards—to force him to trade me. The story began to get a lot of play all over the country, and to tell you the truth, I was amused enough not to correct it .

I was planning to shave it before our last game in Seattle, but coach Bobby Cox reminded me that the catcher's mask might irritate my freshly shaved skin. He was right, so I decided not to shave it until we got to Syracuse for the annual exhibition game. Of course, the beard was none of the writers' business. But I enjoyed watching them scamper around, reading one another's notebooks, concocting all sorts of reasons for the beard.

Inevitably, Billy came to me at the end of the Seattle series and told me he'd been ordered to get me to shave or he was in trouble.

Well, I decided the hell with them,, I was tired of being

put in the middle. And making Billy's future dependent on my shaving was just going too far. There was no way in the world I'd shave under those circumstances.

In Syracuse, I talked to my wife on the phone. She was crying. All the stories about my defying Steinbrenner had gotten to her. Diana and the kids are my weakness—if it had moved her to tears, it was time to take it off.

I asked a friend to go to the lobby of our hotel and buy me some blades. Naturally, the newspapermen overheard him making the purchase, and when he told them I was shaving, I quickly got the inevitable knock on the door.

When I opened it, there were two writers asking if they could come in and watch me shave. I couldn't believe it. At that point, I decided I'd spoken to my full quota of writers for the year. Any time I was asked a question for the rest of the season, all I'd say was "I'm just happy to be here."

We moved into first place on August 23, after winning six of seven on the road, Mike Torrez having won his seventh straight complete game.

We kept playing good ball, and as the division championship moved closer to our grasp, all our problems seemed to recede for the time being.

I started to emerge from my slump in September. I had a personal goal—I wanted to drive in 100 runs and hit .300 for the third consecutive year. It's a feat that has been accomplished very few times in the past few decades. I'd have done it easily with any kind of production in August, but that month was a virtual wipeout. On September 4, we won our seventh straight game, as Don Gullett hurled his first shutout and Heathcliff Johnson hit a grand slam. I had given Cliff the nickname Heathcliff after a comic character, and it really caught on.

By the time the Red Sox came to New York in September, it was pretty much all over. We beat them 4–2 in the opener behind Guidry with more than 55,000 fans at the park on a Tuesday night. On Wednesday night, Figueroa stopped

Boston 2–0. Jackson had a two-run homer off Reggie Cleveland in the ninth. Although we lost 7–3 the next night, we had buried the Sox, and the race was all but over.

We didn't actually clinch the division title until October 1, the next-to-last day of the season. It was raining in New York, and our game against Detroit was held up, so we sat in the clubhouse and watched Baltimore beat Boston. That loss eliminated the Red Sox and made us champions. Elliott Maddox caught the last out for the Orioles.

I was proud of the way I closed the season in those big September games. I wound up hitting safely in my last thirteen in a row for the longest hitting streak of my career. And I had twenty-seven hits in fifty-four at-bats in those games, a .500 average, and lifted my season average from .288 to .308. In ten of the thirteen games, I had two or more hits.

I drove in eleven runs in the thirteen games to give me an even 100 for the season, the third year in a row I'd reached that figure. And I wound up hitting eighteen home runs, my second-highest figure ever.

We won the division in spite of a season to frazzle the nerves of the best of us. We won because we were the strongest team, and in the end, our talent prevailed. They say most hitters will find their own levels by the end of the season, and the same can be said for a team. After 162 games, we were just too good to be denied. Had we been lacking in talent, the inner turmoils would certainly have done us in.

ANOTHER CLOSE ENCOUNTER OF THE ROYAL KIND

In 1976, we had gone into the World Series as a tired team. We tried not to fall into the same trap during the postseason games of 1977; but, sure enough, we were the last of the four teams to clinch our division, and there was little time to rest the regulars for the Championship Series against Kansas City.

Besides, we were a team of virtually only nineteen players. The sale of Carlos May to the Angels in mid-September had left us with a twenty-four-man roster, and efforts to replace him with either Kingman or Del Alston were futile. Besides, we were carrying Mickey Klutts, George Zeber, Ken Holtzman, Fran Healy, and Ken Clay, each of whom Billy was very seldom using.

The bad feelings between the Yankees and the Royals persisted through our second playoff series. They were still peeved about the postponed game they were forced to return for. And there was still the Gura-Martin feud, intensified when Billy suggested he protect Gura on the way to the park to make sure he didn't get hurt.

George Brett wasn't a big fan of the Yankees, either. He

thought the Yankees hadn't given his brother Ken a fair shake the year before. Tempers ran high throughout the playoffs, with hard slides and close pitches adding to the tension of each game.

We opened in New York on the afternoon of Wednesday, October 5. It was really nice to play in the crisp autumn daylight, and the ballpark looked beautiful with the big crowd and the pennants flying.

As in the 1976 race, this home series was the one to win. We needed to beat the Royals not only to get into the World Series, but also to make up for our embarrassing performance in the World Series the year before.

Paul Splittorff opened against us, and it was his day. Don Gullett, complaining of arm trouble, lasted only two innings. Hal McRae hit an early homer, John Mayberry and Al Cowens later connected off Dick Tidrow, and we lost 7–2. Our only scoring was my two-run homer in the third inning.

The second game was a different story. Ron Guidry was in command for this one, as he went all the way to stop the Royals 6–2. I had three of our ten hits, and Cliff Johnson had a big home run. That sent us off to Kansas City, where we needed two out of three for the pennant.

On Friday, we went against Dennis Leonard, and the Royals shone again. He allowed only four hits and a walk in beating us 6–2. Roy White, with two doubles, was the only man able to handle Leonard. I was 0 for four.

Now we needed two in a row on the road, and we were depending on Figueroa. Billy used strong psychology on Gura, almost daring him to beat us, and after allowing four runs and six hits in two innings, Gura was gone.

Figueroa got knocked out in the fourth. Our 5–4 lead wasn't much, but our backs were to the wall, as they say, and it was all we had to cling to.

After Tidrow faced three batters, Sparky came in. The fourth inning is early for Lyle, but he's our best pitcher in clutch situations, and he was up to the task. Sparky closed the door on the Kansas City hitters for five and a third innings, allowing only two hits and no walks, and we came out of the park with a 6–4 win and the series tied. He had been a lifesaver and this victory made it all the more proper that he should win the Cy Young Award.

Guidry was our fifth game pitcher, Splittorff theirs. Everything rested on this final game, just as it had the year before when Chambliss had won it for us in the ninth.

The Royals scored twice in the first inning, as Guidry worked with only two days' rest. Brett and Nettles had a fight over a tag play at third and both benches emptied, but order was restored quickly.

Our lineup had Paul Blair in right, since Martin made the gutsy decision to sit Jackson down. Reggie had not played well in the field, and was only one for fourteen in the series. He was really embarrassed by the benching—and you can bet George was in shock over it—but Martin decided that if this was to be his last game as Yankee manager, he was going to go out on his own terms.

We got a run in the third, but the Royals scored again in their half of the inning and knocked Guidry out. In came Torrez, on one day's rest—we continued to trail 3–1 through seven innings.

In the eighth, we got Splittorff out of there. Herzog brought in Doug Bird, the best relief pitcher the Royals had. But Billy managed to maneuver Herzog into retiring Bird after only a third of an inning. In came Mingori.

It was as though Billy had been prepared for these last two innings all of his managing career. He now had Reggie Jackson pinch-hit and Reggie came through with a big single to cut their lead to 3–2.

Herzog didn't want Mingori pitching in the ninth. Looking back, he probably wished he still had Bird. So he opened the inning with Dennis Leonard, and we opened the inning with a big single from Paul Blair, Jackson's replacement.

Tying run on first. Roy White batted for Dent and drew a walk. Out came Leonard, and in came Gura. Herzog was running out of moves.

Mickey Rivers greeted Gura with a base hit as Blair danced around the bases and we started to go crazy. Now we had two on with no one out in a tie game. Gura came out, and Mark Littell, who had given up Chambliss' homer the year before, relieved. He faced Willie Randolph, and Willie hit a sacrifice fly to score White with the lead run. We were up 4-3.

It wasn't over yet. Brett made a throwing error to let another run score, and we went to the last of the ninth leading 5-3. Sparky had relieved Torrez in the eighth, and was in line to win his second game in two days.

He gave up a one-out single to Frank White, but then Fred Patek hit into a double play, and the series was over. We were winners again, and for the second year in a row, had gone to the ninth inning of the final game before wrapping it up.

We had a wild clubhouse celebration—Billy poured champagne over Steinbrenner and said, "That's for trying to fire me."

I can't remember ever being so emotionally drained. That was one of the hardest series and hardest games I'd ever played in. The thought of dragging our bodies onto the field again was almost too much to ponder at that moment, but we sure wanted to get even for the World Series of the year before. I was only sorry the Reds hadn't made it—I would love to have gotten even with them.

THE DODGERS FALL

We had only two days off between the Championship Series and the World Series—not enough time for the fans to be able to see both clubs at top strength. An extra day or two would enable both clubs to open with their best pitchers. Furthermore, the Dodgers had beaten Philadelphia in four games, and had an extra day's rest on us.

Don Gullett was a surprise starter for us. Most people thought he was through for the season after he left the first playoff game. Otherwise, our lineup was set. Reggie would play every day, and Roy White would sit this one out. Roy had slumped in September, so Piniella was in left field, and we couldn't have a designated hitter in the series.

Don was all psyched up for the game, and he overthrew in the beginning. The Dodgers got two runs in the top of the first, and we had Tidrow warming up right away in the bullpen. I visited Gullett on the mound, and he showed me he was full of confidence. As soon as he settled down, he was fine. In the last of the first, I singled and came around to score on a single by Chambliss. It was my record seventh straight hit in the World Series, carrying over from the pre-

vious season, and then, in the sixth inning, I hit Don Sutton's first pitch to left for a double, tying the game and
knocking Sutton out of the box.

We took a 3–2 lead in the eighth, but Gullett couldn't get
through the ninth and yielded to Lyle, who gave up a game-
tying single to Lee Lacy. But Sparky recovered brilliantly,
shutting out Los Angeles in the tenth, eleventh, and
twelfth innings, until we scored in the last of the twelfth.
Randolph doubled, I was walked intentionally, and Blair,
who had replaced Jackson for defensive reasons, singled to
left for the game winner.

The second game found Catfish on the mound for us, Burt
Hooton for the Dodgers. Hunter hadn't pitched in a month,
but we had no one else to turn to. Cat told his son, "Make
sure you watch the first inning, because I may be gone by
the second." He was almost right. He actually lasted until
the third, but he allowed three home runs, and we were out
of it in a hurry. The Dodgers won 6–1 and evened the Series.

We were our old selves on the trip to Los Angeles. Everybody was mad about ticket locations for our families, Mickey Rivers wanted to be traded, Mike Torrez was talking
about pitching for Boston next year, people asked me about
playing for Cleveland, and Billy was explaining his statements about wanting a new contract if we won.

But once we took the field, we were in command. We
touched Tommy John for five runs and nine hits in six innings, and Torrez pitched a super game for us. We came out
on top 5–3. This meant the Dodgers had to win three out of
four to beat us, contending with the fact that we'd just beat-
en them on their own turf.

Ron Guidry was rested for the fourth game, and he
turned out to be the Guidry we'd known all season. We won
this one 4–2 on a four-hitter, with Reggie hitting a homer,
and we were now just one win away from the World Championship.

I gave some thought to the advantages of winning on the road. If we could wrap it up in Los Angeles, we'd celebrate just among ourselves. No fans would pour onto the field, and we could have a peaceful flight home basking in satisfaction.

Of course, it's glorious to win at home, but the thought of all those fans coming at us is a little frightening. All things considered, I'd have been delighted to wrap it up in Los Angeles the next day.

Gullett was our pitcher and Sutton theirs, a repeat of the first game. But this time, Gullett had some trouble with his control, and the Dodgers jumped all over him, running up a 10–0 lead after six innings.

We got two in the seventh and two in the eighth when Reggie and I hit back-to-back home runs.

As I rounded the bases, Sutton yelled to me, "Is that as hard as you can hit it?" I just laughed. Don and I have a good respect for each other, and I knew what it was like to be embarrassed in the series. Besides, I held no bad feelings toward the Dodgers at all. Cliff Johnson caught the ninth inning, the first inning I'd missed since the last day of the regular season. I was tired, hurting a little, and glad to have an inning off.

Back in New York for the sixth game, it was Torrez against Hooton. It was a nice enough evening, not chilly enough to cause problems, and the park was packed.

The Dodgers scored twice in the first inning, but we tied it in the second. The Dodgers increased it to 3–2, and then, in the last of the fourth, I opened with a single to run my World Series hitting streak to ten. Jackson, hitting behind me, homered to right and put us on top. We added another run and led 5–3 after four.

In the fifth, we got two more off Elias Sosa, as Reggie poked his fourth homer of the series and second in two innings. The place went wild, and despite all the problems between Reggie and his manager and teammates, everyone was in love with him now. He made a curtain call from the dugout, and with the score 7–3 and Torrez pitching well, it looked as though we were on our way.

In the eighth, the fans gave Reggie a standing ovation as he came to bat, and he responded by hitting his third home run of the game. Yankee Stadium had never seen such a performance. What a hero! If only he would limit his act to brilliance on the field, I could really love the man. Anybody who can produce for my team that way can be a teammate of mine any time. It's a shame Reggie doesn't just let his bat do all his talking for him.

We won the game 8–4, and were World Champions. It was our third clubhouse celebration in two weeks, and the sweetest of them all. Our announcer Bill White, who was working for ABC, tried to get me to talk in the postgame interview about Cleveland and my plans for next year, but it was neither the time nor the place. I wanted to enjoy the moment of ultimate triumph. You never know if it will ever come again.

EAT YOUR HEART OUT, FISK!

Guess who did a TV commercial?

I did. Early in 1978, I was asked if I'd do a commercial for *Williams' Lectric Shave*. The theme of the commercial was "Not just another pretty face," which I certainly qualified for, and I was rather pleased with the way it turned out.

Eat your heart out, Fisk.

I remained torn between playing and quitting for much of the winter of 1978, but shortly before spring training, I resigned myself to the situation.

I hadn't been able to move to the Indians. There was no doubt in my mind that I wanted to go with them. My confusion was over whether to quit or play for the Yankees again. And when it came time to make the decision, my continuing love for playing baseball made me realize what I should do.

As long as baseball continued to be fun for me, and as long as I continued to play it well, it was too important to give up. The problems with the front office and the press aside, I still was in love with the two or three hours on the field each day.

People speculated over whether my talk of retiring was a bluff. Hell, no, it wasn't. There were days when I was sure I'd never play again for the Yankees. And there were days I realized how much I'd miss the game. In the end, I knew I had to play.

And as things developed, it all began to fall nicely into place for me. George visited me in Canton during the winter. He seemed out of touch with my real feelings, as I was still upset over old contract misunderstandings. But he came away impressed with my business interests and seemed to feel I was determined to stay with the Yankees.

In spring training, we talked again, and eventually I signed yet another contract. This one satisfied me and my family, and made it possible to put that sore point behind me. It shouldn't have been necessary to go through all that to get where I am now, but I'm assured of playing for the Yankees through the 1981 season, barring a trade. And yes, a trade to Cleveland would still please me.

I have a new love to make things somewhat more pleasant for me this year—airplanes. I studied for my pilot's license and received it during the winter. Now in my twin-engine six-seater Beechcraft Duke, it's possible to fly from New York to Canton in about an hour, and I frequently go home even during home stands.

There was still the usual chaos among the Yankees as the season unfolded. Four players, including myself, skipped a team luncheon and George fined us $500 each. He tried to play a less active role in 1978, handing the day-to-day responsibilities to new team president Al Rosen, but his presence was, of course, always felt.

Even Billy and I had some words on a flight, which just goes to show how the pressures of the game can catch up with you. I was kidding Billy, as I often do, but he was in a sensitive mood, and we had a little argument. By the next day it was forgotten, although, of course, the newspapers made a big deal of it.

As for my going to Cleveland, that may have been held up by the Commissioner's ban on transactions between the two teams. Gabe Paul still retained some of his Yankee stock, and until he could divest himself of it, the Yanks and Indians couldn't make trades. Whether my going to Cleveland could be affected by this arrangement, who could tell? The Indians still seemed unable to come up with anything that would make the Yankees feel they were making a good deal.

I had some injury problems with my feet and legs, and I hope the strain of regular catching for ten professional seasons isn't beginning to take its toll. I enjoy the action behind the plate, and I hope I don't have to consider moving elsewhere to prolong my career.

The Yankees got off to a good start in 1978, but it was obvious that Boston would be strong, and we'd have another dogfight with them. That's great—it keeps the rivalry as strong as ever. And Ralph Houk's Tigers were obviously a coming power, too.

I didn't get off as fast as I would have liked with the bat. By late May, I had hit only one home run, but I was lifting my average and starting to drive in runs, so I felt I'd have a good season after all.

My new home in Canton is now completed. This will help my family feel more settled.

In May, I was honored as the Baseball Father of the Year in advance of Father's Day. It was a nice honor for the man with the grumpy, grouchy reputation.

I'm still not talking to the writers, and we're all feeling better for it. They say hello, I say hello. They don't ask dumb questions, and I don't give them rude answers. Best of all, they don't bring up Cleveland, Steinbrenner, Jackson, contracts, and Fisk all the time, and I'm feeling more mellow as a result. I think it's working out for the best, and in some ways, I'm actually enjoying the season as I used to.

Why not? I may be around here for a long time after all.

CONCLUSION

Although I'm best known to people as a baseball player, I have become fully conscious that baseball represents at best one-third of my interests. My family comes first—Diana, Tracy, Kelly, and Mike mean more to me than a World Championship ever could. Once I became a family man, baseball became the means toward securing their welfare, so that we could have a long and happy life together.

When I was a boy and my father was gone a lot, we didn't have the closest of families. I didn't realize at the time that his absence bothered me, but today I'm sure a lot of my feelings for a close family stem from those early years. I know I'm not the only guy in the world whose occupation keeps him away from home, but I can't help it if it bothers me more than others.

My business interests are as important to me as baseball is. I get tremendous satisfaction out of the buying and selling of real estate. I'd rather be working on figures, stocks, real estate, houses, commercial ground, shopping centers, banks, and restaurants than watching television. I'm proud of my ability to converse with people in almost any field, and proud of my ability to learn quickly when I discover something that interests me.

Baseball is a great conversation opener, but I want to be able to relate to tax people, insurance people, and real estate people on an equal basis. And I love the feeling of being able to say, "I own that."

During the 1977 season, I read a column which compared me to catchers in the Hall of Fame—Mickey Cochrane, Gabby Hartnett, Bill Dickey, Yogi Berra, and Roy Campanella. I never studied them, so I don't know if I'm up there yet, but it was an honor to be counted among them.

I don't want to minimize the importance of baseball to me. I've devoted my entire adult life to the game. It's given me everything I own, plus intangible things like pride and enjoyment. I love the game, and I had a long love affair with the Yankees.

But the onetime pride of being a Yankee is fading. When you go through the kinds of things I went through in 1977, it's hard to think of Lou Gehrig in *Pride of the Yankees* and relate to it. More than ever before, the Yankees have become an employer, and the employee-employer conflicts have taken the enjoyment out of the game for me.

I've worked hard to earn what I've earned, and I'll continue to do things just that way. I could never approach a baseball game or a business deal with less than a 100-percent effort.

If I can be remembered as a "player of the '70s," I'll be proud. I'd like to think that today's players have left the ranks of the dumb jocks and become well-respected individuals, able to fend for themselves in the free enterprise system.

EPILOGUE
by Martin Appel

That Munson, he was never wrong.

When we were finishing our work on this book early in 1978, he told me that it was obvious another tough pennant race was on hand, with the Yankees and Boston battling it out. As I read the final proofs in July, the Yankees were out of the race, some fourteen games behind Boston, and the Red Sox looked like the best team of the century. I thought about taking the paragraph out to save Thurman the embarrassment of a bad prediction, but it was, after all, his book, and he said to leave it in.

The Yankees, 47–42 on July 18, went on to compile a 53–21 record for the balance of the season, staging the comeback of the century. They went to Boston in early September, already having cut the lead to four games, and swept the Sox by scores of 15–3, 13–2, 7–0 and 7–4. Boston recovered but the Yankees held on. A loss on the final day of the season, coupled with a Red Sox victory, set the stage for a historic playoff game in Fenway Park to decide the Eastern Division championship. In one of the most thrilling games ever played, the Yankees edged the Red Sox 5–4, highlighted by a Bucky Dent home run, and the division was won.

Riding high, the Yankees rolled over Kansas City, at last enjoying a relatively easy Championship Series, taking their third straight American League pennant in four games.

In the World Series, this team of destiny lost the first two games and then came back to win four straight—the first time that had ever been accomplished. The Yankees, for the second year in a row, were World Champions, and the 1978 season will live for all ages.

The season marked an apparent slowing down of Munson's career. While still one of the most feared clutch hitters in all of baseball, his mighty offensive figures slipped a bit. His streak of three consecutive .300 seasons with 100 or more RBIs came to an end, and his home run output fell from eighteen to six. Still, he batted .297, and showed amazing durability by appearing in 154 games.

It wasn't age that was catching up with Munson; it was the beating his body had taken after eleven professional seasons as a catcher. He spent most of the year in pain. His knees were so sore that in July, Billy Martin acknowledged the hopelessness of the situation and moved Thurman to the outfield.

Never a good defensive player out there, for lack of experience certainly, Munson accepted the move with understanding. The pain had gotten to him, and he was facing the inevitable.

But after thirteen games, he was feeling bouncy again. The amazing events of Martin's firing, Bob Lemon's hiring and Martin's rehiring for 1980 all coincided with this period, and Munson soon returned to his usual position behind the plate. It was around this time that the Yankee express began to roll, and even if Munson wasn't driving in the runs with his old frequency, he was certainly contributing timely hits and was handling the pitching staff as no one in baseball could.

The rebirth of Catfish Hunter was essential to the Yankee comeback, and Hunter gave credit to Munson.

The relief pitching of Goose Gossage was phenomenal, and Gossage gave credit to Munson.

The work of Ron Guidry could not be described, other

than to say that he enjoyed the best season of any pitcher in this century. He gave credit to Munson.

Had Thurman been hurting the club, he'd have told Lemon and taken himself out. But Thurman never lost the cocky self-confidence, and he knew that with the game on the line, he was the man he wanted up there.

He was hit in the head with a pitch that sent fright through the entire Yankee organization. A day later, he was back. People were ready to write him off for the season.

He was hit in the throat with a foul ball. He coughed, cleared his throat, and kept catching. People were ready to write him off for the season.

In that final game of the regular season, lost to Cleveland to send matters into a playoff situation, Munson raced home from first on a first-inning single with as daring a bit of base running as you'd ever want to see, aching legs and all. It was the first run of the game, and had it been the only run, it would have won a division title and been remembered as one of the great plays in baseball history. Alas, great plays are sometimes lost to circumstance, and when the Yankees lost the game, Munson's play was lost to history.

In the playoffs he hit a game-winning home run and batted .278 for a lifetime Championship Series average of .339. In the World Series he drove in seven runs, including five in one game, and batted .320 for a lifetime World Series average of .373, among the highest in baseball history.

And after the season was over, he took his aching body home to Canton and had surgery on his right shoulder to alleviate friction in the acromioclavicular joint. Surgery was one of the few things Munson didn't handle by himself.

All through the 1978 season, Munson kept pretty much to himself. All he ever had to say to the press was "I'm just happy to be here," which they found insulting. But Munson found it relaxing, and he was happier than he had been in

years, despite the continued turmoils and controversies
raging around him. He was still the team captain, but
somehow, he let silent leadership prevail and managed to
avoid being in the eye of the storm.

Every now and then, a reporter might find himself alone
with Munson in the Yankee clubhouse. Fearful of his bark,
the reporter might approach politely. The result would be
either a fierce rejection or a warm exchange. Munson
remained an enigma to the press, but he knew it and in a
way enjoyed the mystery.

Thurman's relationship with the press didn't bother the
fans. Another player's might, but they saw through to
Thurman and they loved him. Yankee Stadium fans
greeted him with consistent ovations, and they knew the
pain he was playing with. They knew it despite the fact
that he never spoke of it in public.

At a dinner in Ohio during the winter, Thurman helped
to raise $70,000 for a charity. But it was a men-only affair,
and when a woman reporter broke in to interview Thurman, he let her know she wasn't welcome. The story got
national attention, but nowhere was it mentioned that he
was helping to raise $70,000 for charity.

During spring training of 1979, Jim Bouton of Channel 2
in New York persisted in trying to get an interview with
Munson. He kept the cameras rolling as he followed
Munson around the batting cage until Thurman, harrassed
long enough, shoved the microphone away and berated the
former Yankee player. Bouton ran the tape that night, as
though to demonstrate how obnoxious Munson could be.
The fans saw it the other way around and rallied to
Munson's support. He was still the "people's choice."

Munson's devotion to his family never wavered. Young
Mike was having a hard time settling down, and Munson
recognized his need for attention. If possible, this problem
drew him even closer to the home.

When we first worked on this book, Thurman was

reluctant to discuss flying. He hadn't quite worked out an understanding with George Steinbrenner on it. But eventually he did. George wasn't about to trade Munson to Cleveland, so he agreed to Thurman's request that he receive permission to fly home to be with his family.

Munson loved his plane and took to it as he took to real estate, investments, anything he set his mind to. Soon he was commuting home after night games, returning the next day. By 1979 he didn't even bother to rent a place in New York. If he had to be in New York the next day, he'd stay overnight with a teammate. But usually he went home.

The surgery performed on Thurman during the off-season seemed to work. His arm felt good, and he was throwing with traces of his old brilliance. In 1979, as in 1978, he remained high in popularity, low among the press, and managed to stay out of the controversies that somehow always seemed to follow the Yankees.

But his legs were aching again. And the pain was showing up in different ways. The long games took their toll, and the days of catching doubleheaders and day games after night games were gone.

The Yankees made some movies to acquire backup protection but no moves to get a number one catcher to take over for Thurman. It seemed clear that with his aches after 1,400 major league games, Thurman had left the peak years of his career behind him.

Indeed, an era ended in July when neither Munson nor Carlton Fisk was voted to the All-Star team; the honor went to Darrell Porter.

With Munson, at 32, in pain; with Roy White, Lou Piniella, Reggie Jackson, Graig Nettles, Chris Chambliss, Catfish Hunter and Jim Spencer all in "middle age" by baseball years, it seemed as though the Yankees were an old team. Lemon was replaced by the resilient Billy Martin in June, and Mickey Rivers and Dick Tidrow were traded.

The modern dynasty that had begun with White in 1965 and Munson in 1969 was now the old guard, which was beginning to pass.

Thurman bought a new plane in 1979—a jet, no less. It was a $1.3 million twin-engine Cessna Citation, registered as 15NY, and it was a big advancement over his previous aircraft. Although he had had his pilot's license for better than a year and a half, he couldn't take over an aircraft like this without some lessons.

His teammates, to whom he would show off the plane, always kidded him about the risks. Baseball humor is frequently in questionable taste, but Munson always said he was safer in his plane than others were in cars.

As July turned to August, Munson yielded his catching spot to rookie Jerry Narron. The pain in his legs was, even for Munson, too much. He told Billy Martin that he wasn't helping much behind the plate.

The papers said he would never catch again, but the next day he was back behind the plate. It was only temporary however, and his regular days as a catcher did seem to have passed.

When Chambliss suffered an injury, Munson was placed at first base, another out-of-position spot for him, but being the natural athlete that he was, he adjusted. His future was quite questionable at this juncture. First base certainly wasn't available when Chambliss returned, catching was becoming difficult, the outfield was overcrowded and hazardous. Munson was at the very crossroads of his career.

His production at the plate was well off his top years. Although his batting average was up near .290, his power was gone and the RBIs were not so frequent. There was some talk of Chambliss being traded to let Munson move to first, but around the Yankees there was always talk about something.

The Yankees were seemingly well out of the pennant

race after dropping three straight in Milwaukee in late July. Following the loss on Sunday, July 29, Thurman and his father-in-law Tony Dominick flew home for his son Mike's fourth birthday. The next day he met the team in Chicago where they got the three back. On August 1, Thurman's last game, he played first and batted third but left the game in the third inning with an aggravated knee.

That was a Wednesday night. With the next game not scheduled until Friday night in New York, Thurman went home to Canton as he always did.

It was a time for family. On Thursday afternoon, August 2, he told his father-in-law that he was having some problems with his new plane, and he wanted to check it out.

He met his flight instructor, David Hall, and another friend, Jerry Anderson, at the Akron-Canton Airport. They took the plane up to find the problem and practice takeoffs and landings.

The weather was not a problem, but apparently the plane was, at least for Munson. There was an embankment at the end of runway 19, and Munson was at least 40 feet too low over it. The plane scraped some trees and the wings were sheared off. With little control over the plane, there was not much hope. The jet came in 1,000 feet short of the runway, bouncing some 500 feet to Greensburg Road, outside the airport.

Hall and Anderson got out and tried to pull Thurman out too. But stored jet fuel suddenly ignited, and the men's clothing caught fire. They were forced back from the fiery wreckage, making further rescue attempts impossible.

Thurman lived in a world of bottled up emotions, but no one held back when the news was released. George Steinbrenner cried. Billy Martin cried. The nation was stunned, not just the sports world, but the whole nation; the story was page one news. Here was an athlete of 32, with everything to live for, dead before his time.

The last time I saw Thurman was twelve days before he died. He told me about the plane, and he told me about Tracy, Kelly and Mike. He asked when my wife was expecting our first child, and he said we'd have to get together after the season. He asked me if he could still get some copies of this book for people back in Canton. His mind was still back home.

With his death, people talked about Thurman Munson entering the Hall of Fame, as Roberto Clemente had when a plane crash took his life. I had never thought about it much, for it seemed that Thurman might play for another five or six years before one could properly evaluate his credentials. But now we at the Baseball Commissioner's office were forced to evaluate them early, and they looked good.

A Rookie of the Year and a Most Valuable Player. A .300 hitter five times. Three consecutive years of 100 RBIs and a .300 average. The captain of a three-time pennant winning and two-time World Championship club. A dominant man at his position for a decade. A record setter in both Championship Series and World Series play. Certainly enough there to fill up a plaque.

But as Munson would tell you, his baseball career was only one side of him. His business side was also a success story, both for the financial growth and acquired wealth, and for the way he taught himself how to do it.

And in paying tribute to him, everyone cited his devotion to Diana and the children. The family. If he could have written this whole book about nothing but them, he'd have done it. They were number one.

Sure he was grouchy, and maybe he insulted more than a couple of writers along the way. But he was as honest a man as you could find. He wanted to be remembered as a player of the '70s, and by fate, his career ran from 1969–1979. What he packed into those years was a lifetime for anyone, and the love he gave to those close to him was enough to keep them warm in memories for many, many years.

Thurman never wanted to be captain of the Yankees, but he was the right man at the right time to hold that honor. He brought pride to the organization even when he thought pride was failing. His predecessor as Yankee captain, Lou Gehrig, had died at 37. It will be a long time before anyone holds the office again.

He was a complex man, but the fans knew him better than they thought. They saw his hustle, his pride, his determination, his honesty, his confidence, his dignity and his character. And that was what he was all about both on and off the field.

(The New York Times/Sandra Krulwich)

(The New York Times/Sandra Krulwich)

Yankee Stadium
August 3, 1979

CAREER RECORD OF THURMAN MUNSON

Year Club	G	AB	R	H	2B	3B	HR	RBI	BB	SO	SH	SF	GI DP	HP	SB	CS	AVG	PO	A	E	DP	PB	PCT.
1968 Binghamton	71	226	28	68	12	3	6	37	36	27	0	2	⅃	2	4	6	.301	327	53	9	5	5	.977
1969 Syracuse	28	102	13	37	9	1	2	17	13	11	0	0	—	0	1	1	.363	81	13	6	2	1	.940
New York	26	86	6	22	1	2	1	9	10	10	5	1	5	0	0	1	.256	119	18	2	0	5	.986
1970 New York	132	453	59	137	25	4	6	53	57	56	5	4	13	7	5	7	.302	631	80*	8	11	10	.989
1971 New York	125	451	71	113	15	4	10	42	52	65	4	3	10	7	6	5	.251	547	67	1	4	9	.998*
1972 New York	140	511	54	143	16	3	7	46	47	58	4	2	13	3	6	7	.280	575	71	15*	11	9	.977
1973 New York	147	519	80	156	29	2	20	74	48	64	1	4	12	4	4	6	.301	673	80*	12	11*	10	.984
1974 New York	144	517	64	135	19	2	13	60	44	66	1	8	14	1	2	0	.261	743	75*	22*	10	6	.974
1975 New York	157	597	83	190	24	3	12	102	45	51	3	10	23	6	3	2	.318	725	95	23*	14*	9	.973
1976 New York	152	616	79	186	27	1	17	105	29	37	1	10	17	9	14	11	.302	546	78	14	8	12*	.978
1977 New York	149	595	85	183	28	5	18	100	39	55	0	2	18	4	2	6	.308	657	73	12	4	10	.984
1978 New York	154	617	73	183	27	1	6	71	35	70	1	10	20	3	2	3	.297	698	61	11	4	8	.986
1979 New York	97	382	42	110	18	3	3	39	32	37	1	4	15	0	1	2	.288	428	44	10	7	5	.979
M. L. Totals	1423	5344	696	1558	229	32	113	691	438	569	21	58	160	42	54	50	.292	6342	742	130	84	93	.982

CHAMPIONSHIP SERIES RECORD

Year Club	G	AB	R	H	2B	3B	HR	RBI	BB	SO	SH	SF	DP	HP	SB	CS	AVG	PO	A	E	DP	PB	PCT.
1976 vs. K.C.	5	23	3	10	2	0	0	3	0	1	0	0	1	0	0	0	.435	18	6	2	0	1	.923
1977 vs. K.C.	5	21	3	6	1	0	1	5	0	2	0	1	0	0	0	0	.286	25	4	0	0	0	1.000
1978 vs. K.C.	4	18	2	5	1	0	1	2	0	0	0	0	0	0	0	0	.278	22	4	0	0	1	1.000
ALCS Totals	14	62	8	21	4	0	2	10	0	3	0	1	1	0	0	1	.339	64	14	2	0	2	.975

WORLD SERIES RECORD

Year Club	G	AB	R	H	2B	3B	HR	RBI	BB	SO	SH	SF	DP	HP	SB	CS	AVG.	PO	A	E	DP	PB	PCT.
1976 vs. Cin.	4	17	2	9	0	0	0	2	0	1	0	0	0	0	0	0	.529	21	7	0	0	0	1.000
1977 vs. L.A.	6	25	4	8	2	0	1	3	2	8	0	0	1	0	0	0	.320	40	5	0	0	1	1.000
1978 vs. L.A.	6	25	5	8	3	0	0	7	3	7	0	0	1	0	1	0	.320	33	5	0	1	0	1.000
W.S. Totals	16	67	11	25	5	0	1	12	5	16	0	0	2	0	1	1	.373	94	17	0	1	1	1.000

ALL-STAR GAME RECORD

Year Site	G	AB	R	H	2B	3B	HR	RBI	BB	SO	SH	SF	DP	HP	SB	CS	AVG.	PO	A	E	DP	PB	PCT.
1971 Detroit	1	0	0	0	0	0	0	0	0	0	0	0	0	0	0	0	.000	1	0	0	0	0	1.000
1973 Kansas City	1	2	0	0	0	0	0	0	0	0	0	0	0	0	0	0	.000	5	1	0	0	0	1.000
1974 Pittsburgh	1	3	1	1	1	0	0	0	0	0	0	0	0	0	0	0	.333	7	0	1	0	0	.875
1975 Milwaukee	1	2	0	1	0	0	0	0	0	0	0	0	0	1	0	0	.500	1	1	0	0	0	1.000
1976 Philadelphia	1	2	0	0	0	0	0	0	0	0	0	0	0	0	0	0	.000	4	0	0	0	1	1.000
1977 New York	1	1	0	0	0	0	0	0	0	1	0	0	0	0	0	0	.000	0	0	0	0	0	.000
1978 San Diego	(SELECTED; REPLACED DUE TO INJURY)																						
A.S. Totals	6	10	1	2	1	0	0	0	0	2	0	0	0	1	0	0	.200	18	2	1	0	1	.952

abbreviations

G–Games AB–At Bats R–Runs H–Hits 2B–Doubles 3B–Triples HR–Home Runs RBI–Runs Batted In BB–Bases on Balls SO–Strikeouts SH–Sacrifice Hits SF–Sacrifice Flies GIDP–Grounded into Double Plays HP–Hit by Pitch SB–Stolen Bases CS–Caught Stealing AVG.–Batting Average PO–Putouts A–Assists E–Errors DP–Double Plays PB–Passed Balls PCT–Fielding Percentage *–led league *–tied for league lead